Gayle Soucek

Amazon Parrots

Everything About Purchase, Care, Nutrition, Behavior, and Training

BARRON'S

2 CONTENTS

INTRODUCTION TO AMAZONS

Of the approximately 365 known parrot species in the world today, perhaps the most easily recognized are those in the genus **Amazona.** *From the familiar green-feathered presence on a swash-buckling pirate's shoulder to the child's talking toy that squawks out a tinny "Polly wanna cracker," Amazons are an iconic presence in our collective awareness, the archetypal parrot.*

The common perception about Amazons developed in part due to the early and extensive trade in Amazons as companion birds. Amazons were probably not one of the first parrots kept as human pets. That distinction probably belongs to one of the many Asiatic parakeets brought back from India by early Roman explorers more than 2,300 years ago. In truth, New World parrots (those native to the Americas and the Caribbean) were more likely to end up in a stew pot rather than be kept as companions. When European explorers first landed onshore, however, they marveled at the intelligent and colorful birds that had the amazing ability to mimic human speech. Thus began a long, lucrative, and ultimately destructive Amazon pet trade.

Genus Amazona

The genus *Amazona* encompasses approximately 30 species and numerous subspecies ranging from South and Central America to the Caribbean Islands and parts of Mexico. Although no Amazon parrots are native to the United States, some feral populations of escaped or abandoned pets have been reported in Texas, Florida, and California. Because taxonomy is a rapidly evolving science, the number of recognized Amazon species differs depending on the source. Ornithologist Joseph Forshaw describes 27, ornithologist Tony Jupiter describes 31, and Wikipedia lists 32. The Amazona Society, which is a worldwide group of Amazon breeders and fanciers, describes 30 living species and 32 subspecies. A few not listed, including the Martinique Amazon and the Guadeloupe Amazon, are now extinct. Other species are critically endangered and should not be kept as pets. In all, only about 10 species make up the bulk of companion Amazons commonly available in captivity.

Amazons in the Wild

In the wild, Amazons range widely throughout tropical rain forests, swamplands, and savannahs. They roost in huge flocks that can number hundreds of birds. During the day,

however, mated pairs and sometimes their offspring fly long distances to hunt for food. Amazons are opportunistic feeders that will eat almost anything. Their typical diet, though, consists of seeds, fruits, buds, and nuts. In settled areas, Amazons can cause great damage to grain crops and fruit plantations, and they are often chased or killed by farmers.

Amazons are cavity nesters that make their nests in old woodpecker holes, rotted tree trunks, or crevices in rocks. The female lays 2–4 white eggs, although usually not all the chicks survive. The female does most of the incubation, while the male feeds her and guards the nest. Once the eggs hatch after about 26 days, the male will also help feed the chicks. Amazon chicks are altricial, which means they are born naked, helpless, and blind. They are cared for around the clock by both parents until they are ready to venture out of the nest at about ten weeks of age. At that point, the father will typically continue to feed them if they beg, but the mother will often be ready for them to move out. The parents and chicks will usually remain in a family group for quite a bit longer, however. The older youngsters might even help baby sit younger siblings when the parents return to nest.

Conservation Issues

Although Amazons were once common and wide ranging, they have been subjected to intense pressures that have greatly reduced their numbers. In fact, at this point, virtually all of the island species are endangered and at risk of extinction. The other species are threatened or at least require careful conservation management. In response to the overwhelming

pressures from the pet trade, the United States government passed the Wild Bird Conservation Act of 1992. It effectively prohibited the importation of almost all parrot species, except under special permit to groups such as zoos and research facilities. By the 1990s, much of the damage was already done.

For example, in the eight-year period from 1983 through 1990, over 300,000 Blue-fronted Amazons were legally exported from Argentina alone. That does not include birds exported from nearby countries. It also does not include the estimated 50,000 or so a year that were exported illegally or smuggled. Unfortunately, these statistics are for just one species of Amazon.

The pet trade, however, was not alone in decimating wild populations. During those same years, huge tracts of rain forest were clear-cut to create agricultural land. Cavity-nesting birds such as parrots were deprived of trees for breeding sites, killed as crop pests, and crowded into smaller and less-hospitable habitats. Island parrots faced the same challenges in addition to natural disasters such as hurricanes that destroyed their already-limited habitat. Scientists and local governments are now working to reverse some of the damage with species management plans, but it is likely too late for some species.

Captive-Bred Amazons

Luckily, many of those imported Amazons found their way into captive-breeding programs. Some species have flourished. Blue-fronts and the several members of the Yellow-headed *A. ochrocephala* group are readily available as pets, as are many other

less-common captive species. The more vulnerable and endangered species are not available—or at least should not be available—in the pet trade.

The Amazon Personality

Amazons are typically extroverted and boisterous. They are curious and extremely intelligent. They usually mimic human speech well. Amazons do not do anything in a small way. They usually love drama, either as the spectator or as the cause! Some individuals can be shy. More often, though, they love to show off and become the center of attention. In fact, Amazons are one of the few parrot species that will readily talk in front of strangers. African gray parrots might develop a larger vocabulary and clearer speaking voice. Usually no one outside the gray's owner and family

will ever hear it speak, though. The same is not true with Amazons; the world is their stage.

Amazons can be strong willed and stubborn. Mature birds often become temperamental during breeding season, even without a mate. They are also loud. Amazons are generally not a good choice if you live in an apartment or have nearby neighbors with sensitive ears. However, once you gain an Amazon's affection and trust, you will likely have a loyal and loving companion for many, many years. Their average life span is about 50 years in captivity, but octogenarian Amazons are not uncommon.

Is an Amazon Right for You?

A pet Amazon should never be an impulse purchase. You will be committing to a companion that has a potential life span close to that of humans, an intellect similar to a

CHECKLIST

Ask Yourself

✔ Do I have the time to interact and play with my Amazon daily?

✔ Do I have the space for a large cage, play stand, pet carrier, food containers, and all the other paraphernalia that parrots require?

✔ Do I have the money to provide all the necessities, including fresh food, toys, and regular or emergency veterinary care?

✔ Can I tolerate the noise and some inevitable mess from tossed food, molted feathers, and chewed papers?

✔ Is my family on board with the decision, or will the bird's needs be a source of resentment or arguments?

✔ Do I have other pets? Amazons often get along well with dogs and some cats but should never be left unsupervised with them. Snakes and ferrets can pose a serious risk and must always be securely caged around a parrot.

✔ Do I have small children that might tease or torment the Amazon? Amazons have long memories and sharp beaks. Children must learn to act appropriately around a parrot.

✔ Do I understand this is a long-term commitment and not a pet that will live for just a few years?

people want a "talking bird" because they think it will be cool and amusing, only to find themselves overwhelmed and frustrated at the care required. Know what you are getting into!

Once you have carefully considered the "Ask Yourself" questions, you will know if an Amazon is the right pet for your household. If the answer is "Yes," congratulations! You are on the way to a remarkable relationship with a creature that will never fail to amuse and delight you.

five-year-old child, and the emotional age of a human toddler. Parrots are extremely high maintenance pets, requiring a great deal of companionship and interaction. So many

CHOOSING A COMPANION AMAZON

If you have decided that an Amazon is the right pet for you, do your homework carefully before you buy. Baby Amazons are not as plentiful as some other species of parrots, and you might need to search a bit to find exactly what you want.

Although Amazons were imported in huge numbers during the 1980s and early 1990s, they were not commonly set up in breeding programs. This was due in part to their easy availability, relatively cheap price, and undeserved reputation as being difficult to breed in captivity. Once importation was halted, captive breeding became more common. However, many Amazon species are still in short supply in the pet trade.

Baby Birds vs. Adult Amazons

What you might find on the market is an abundance of adult Amazons that are being dumped due to behavioral problems. Of course, the seller will rarely tell you that. You are more likely to hear a tale of woe about how he or she must give up a beloved pet due to financial constraints, family allergies, or unexpected

relocations. The bottom line is that many—although certainly not all—adult pet parrots offered for sale are being abandoned because the owner can no longer handle the bird or live with its behavior.

Bad behavior is not the fault of the parrot! There is no such thing as an inherently bad parrot. Bad behavior is a result of the bird's misguided attempts to fit into a situation it does not understand. With proper socializing and teaching, even the worst-behaved Amazon has the potential to turn into a wonderful companion. Ask yourself if you have the time, resources, patience, and ability to retame and retrain an angry, frightened, or confused parrot and one that possibly has deeply entrenched undesirable habits such as vicious biting or nonstop screaming?

If you are an experienced parrot owner and wish to rescue such a bird, by all means consider adopting an adult Amazon and giving it a new lease on life. You will probably be rewarded with a loving, lifelong companion. If you are a new parrot owner, however, and you are simply estimating the money you would save by buying an older bird, please reconsider. If you are not up to the challenge of buying an adult Amazon, both you and the bird will suffer.

Some parrots are "bouncers" because they tend to move from one home to the next. Each new owner gets lost in the desire to own a beautiful parrot at a cheap price. When the

novelty wears off and the realization sets in that teaching the bird requires a lot work, another "Amazon for sale" ad hits the classifieds. The more they bounce from home to home, the more depressed and distrustful these birds become. The luckiest ones eventually wind up in the hands of experienced parrot owners who love and rehabilitate them. The unlucky ones wind up relegated to back bedrooms or basements with little human contact because their frustrated owners do not know what else to do.

Baby birds on the other hand, come to you straight from a breeder or pet shop. They are too young to have developed any habits—good or bad—and are essentially blank slates waiting to be taught by their new owners. Although this makes them much easier to handle in the beginning, it also places the responsibility on you to raise the baby in a manner that helps it grow into a well-behaved adult. Make sure you do not inadvertently raise a "bouncer"! Later chapters will provide you with more guidance on behavioral training.

Where to Find Amazons

Your best bet is to purchase your pet from an Amazon breeder or from a pet shop that is experienced in caring for large parrots. Local avian veterinarians and bird clubs can probably provide you with resources. You can also check the classified ads in magazines such as *Bird Talk*. The Internet is also a great tool. Websites such as *www.upatsix.com* will bring you into contact with breeders and shops from all across the country. Be very cautious, however, when dealing with people you do not know or whose references you cannot easily confirm. The website Upatsix allows buyers to rate sell-

ers, so shady dealers get weeded out eventually. Unfortunately, that does not prevent them from coming back with different names and addresses.

Although risk is always involved when buying a parrot from a stranger, buying Amazons is especially risky. Amazons are one of the parrots most frequently smuggled into the United States. Besides the obvious violation of federal law, smuggled birds can carry diseases that are deadly to domestic poultry flocks. One such disease, Exotic Newcastle Disease (END), is reportable under law. In other words, if your Amazon tests positive for END, a veterinarian must report the bird to state or federal health authorities. That bird *and any others that have been in contact with it* will be seized

and immediately euthanized. The disease is extremely rare—almost nonexistent—in captive-raised parrots and those that were imported legally and properly quarantined before 1994. However, it can exist in smuggled birds.

If you are ever offered an Amazon with an unknown or questionable background, especially if the seller is quick to sell it for an unusually low price, walk away or at least proceed with extreme caution. Smugglers sometimes will go as far as to bleach the head feathers of common species in order to make them look like more expensive species. If an Amazon's feather coloring, especially head feathers, looks suspicious, or if the feathers show signs of bleaching, decline the sale and notify the police or your local United States

Department of Fish and Wildlife representative. Parrot smuggling is a federal crime and not one the authorities take lightly.

Choosing a Healthy Bird

Once you have found an Amazon, you will want to be sure it is healthy. Spend a few minutes quietly observing the bird from a distance. Parrots are prey animals and will try to hide signs of illness if they know they are being watched. In the wild, sick or weakened birds are the first targets of a predator. So a lot is riding on the bird appearing healthy. Watch for any of the following signs:

✔ Lethargy, disorientation, or a slow reaction to environmental stimuli
✔ Ruffled, dull, or unkempt feathers
✔ Discharge from the eyes, nostrils, or mouth
✔ Slumped posture, especially when the bird is standing on both feet
✔ Labored breathing at rest, especially accompanied by clicking sounds or tail-pumping motion
✔ Vent area pasted with feces

Telling the difference between a healthy but sleepy bird and a bird that is seriously ill is sometimes tricky. Sleepy parrots will often slump down with ruffled feathers and partially closed eyes as they try to grab a nap. The differences can be seen, however, if you take a closer look. Sleepy parrots usually perch on one foot, with the other foot tucked up into their belly feathers. Sick parrots cling to the perch with both feet. Sleepy parrots might appear glassy eyed but will immediately snap to alertness if something catches their interest. A sick parrot might try to appear alert, but usually its eyes still look watery or glazed. Healthy baby parrots might have very rough, frayed, or missing feathers due to their rowdy and clumsy play, but the feathers should still have a bright color and healthy sheen despite the damage. A healthy parrot is bright eyed and curious, and it moves easily about its enclosure.

If you have doubts, come back another day to observe again. The Amazon may just be having a bad day, may be exhausted from play, or may be fearful about something that happened earlier. Most reputable pet stores and breeders will offer some type of health guarantee. However, you do not want to start out with the heartache and trouble of a sick pet. Health guarantees usually require a veterinary exami-

nation within a specified time limit. You must understand and follow the terms carefully, or the guarantee might be voided.

The First Veterinary Visit

Once you purchase your Amazon, take it to an avian veterinarian for an initial checkup. If you have done your homework, you should have a veterinarian already lined up. The pet shop or breeder can make recommendations or check with the Association of Avian Veterinarians for a veterinarian in your area. You can find the association on the Web at *www.aav.org* or can call them at (561) 393-8901. Please be aware that your usual dog and cat veterinarian will probably not be able to treat your bird. Avian medicine is quite different from small-mammal medicine, and few veterinarians specialize in both.

At the first visit, the veterinarian will do a general physical exam and might suggest certain tests and vaccines. Some clinics even offer a discounted "new bird package" that includes the most helpful tests. These are designed to make sure that your Amazon is not suffering from any underlying illness, and to give the veterinarian a healthy baseline for your particular bird. Usual tests include complete blood counts (CBC), fecal exams to check for parasites, Gram's stains to identify dangerous bacteria, and sometimes a blood panel to assess the bird's general health. The doctor will probably weigh the parrot and might perform some grooming, including nail and wing clipping.

This is also a good time to ask questions and discuss any care concerns you might have. Some clinics have a wealth of handouts that provide valuable information for new bird owners. If you are a new client, you should discuss how the veterinarian handles after-hours emergency and who acts as backup if the doctor is out of town.

Bringing Home the Bird

Before you bring home a new Amazon (or any pet, for that matter), prepare in advance for its arrival. Purchase the cage, food, toys, and all necessary supplies before you pick up the bird. Assemble and outfit the cage. Decide where to place it. You should place the cage in an area where your pet can interact easily with the family but not in a spot where it will be stressed with heavy traffic and be unable to rest. In many homes, family rooms are a good choice. Avoid kitchens due to the danger posed by cooking and cleaning fumes. Avoid bedrooms, unless you wish to awakened at the crack of dawn each morning by an exuberant parrot.

If you have other birds, you will need to quarantine the new arrival until you are certain it is healthy. True quarantine is impossible in a normal family home due to airflow constraints and other issues. At least place the newcomer in a temporary spot as far removed from the other birds as possible. Always feed and clean the new Amazon last, and wash your hands carefully when moving between birds. Use a quarantine period of at least 30 days to give any subclinical illness time to show up. Even a long quarantine is no proof that your Amazon is not carrying disease, but it will help weed out some obvious and problematic illnesses.

Once you are fairly confident your new pet is healthy, you can move it into the same room as other birds. Give everyone time to get acquainted, and always supervise interactions between pets. Be aware that parrots, like people, can react with jealousy and dislike. Some might

injure each other in a quest for dominance. Some smaller parrots, such as lovebirds, parrotlets, and Senegals, can be very aggressive with even much larger birds and might provoke a fight they are ill equipped to win.

The first days in a new home are stressful. Your Amazon might greatly miss its siblings or previous human caretakers. Spend time near the bird, talking and interacting, but do not overwhelm it with attention and visitors.

Allow it to settle in and get used to its new surroundings. Take your cues from the bird. Try not to spend either considerably more or considerably less time with it than you expect to spend in the future. The key is to begin acclimating the bird immediately to your typical routine. Parrots are creatures of habit and are happiest once they know what to expect. With the right start, you will be well on your way to a lifelong friendship.

CREATING A
HEALTHY HOME

If a man's home is his castle, then a bird's castle is surely its cage. Even very tame birds usually spend most of their day caged while their owners go off to work or school. For this reason, you should choose the largest and nicest cage you can afford.

A small, poorly built cage can create both physical and emotional problems for your pet. It will likely be a headache for you as well when you attempt to clean or service it. Think of it this way: have you ever spent a week or more traveling and sleeping in a small hotel room? Although it might suit your temporary needs just fine, would you want to spend the rest of your life camped in that tiny place? Your Amazon will feel the same way.

Choosing the Right Cage

Without plenty of room to play, to forage for food, to seek shelter, and to exercise, a pet bird can suffer boredom, depression, and a host of physical problems tied to a lack of mobility.

This does not mean you must provide a massive cage that takes over most of your living space. You should, though, always aim for the largest cage that fits your practical needs.

Cage Size

An old rule of thumb says that a companion bird's cage should average 1½ times the bird's wingspan in dimension. In other words, a large Amazon with a 2-foot (60 cm) wingspan should be in a cage about 3 feet (1 m) wide, deep, and high. Few birdcages are actually designed as perfect cubes, but the idea is to allow for that approximate amount of space. The bird must have room to move about and flap its wings freely. Of course, this is a very general rule and does not take into consider-

Cages and Health

Be aware that your choice of cage can ultimately affect your pet's health and even its life span.

also have a strong tendency toward obesity, you should keep them in a cage large enough to house a variety of perches, swings, and toys comfortably. An Amazon that has just one or two perches, a single toy, and close access to a filled food dish is likely a fat bird. Obesity affects parrots in exactly the same way it affects humans. It puts them at high risk of metabolic diseases such as diabetes, coronary artery disease, and some cancers.

What is an appropriate-size cage? The typical Amazon-sized cage marketed in pet shops and on the Internet is usually about 28–36 inches (66–90 cm) wide, 24–28 inches (60–66 cm) deep, and 34–48 inches (90–120 cm) high. These are suitable. If you have the room and the money for an even larger cage, such as those marketed for cockatoos and macaws, your Amazon will fare better.

Bar Spacing

Bar spacing is an important consideration for small pet birds that can trap their heads and injure themselves between the bars of too-large cages. It is unlikely that any well-manufactured cages exist with bar spacing too large for an Amazon. Be aware of the possibility when considering a homemade or poorly designed imported cage. In general, bar spacing

ation the bird's personality and activity level. Some very active parrot species, such as caiques, should be housed in much larger cages to give them room to romp. Shy and sensitive parrots like many African species often feel more secure in relatively compact cages.

Although young Amazons can be quite active, they have a tendency to become "perch potatoes" as they mature. Because Amazons

for a medium-large parrot cage runs between about ¾ inch (2 cm) up to 1¼ inches (3 cm). With Amazons, bar spacing becomes troublesome only if the bars are too close together. If you place your pet in a cage with bar spacing of less than ¾ inch (2 cm), you very well might come home to find that your feathered darling has managed to get its beak to span two bars and has crimped them together or broken the welds. Wider spacing will prevent this costly and destructive game.

Important Cage Considerations

Parrot cages come in a huge variety of colors, shapes, compositions, and price ranges. You might think you are being frugal by buying the cheapest one on the market, but do your homework and know what you are buying. Surprisingly, sometimes the most-expensive cage is the most economical due to its ease of cleaning and durability. Consider the following.

Is this cage the correct size for my pet, according the above guidelines?

Is it made safely, without sharp edges or crevices that could cut a bird or trap a toe? Run your hand carefully along inside edges to test.

Is it the right material? Wood, plastic, and mesh cages are unsuitable for Amazons, who will chew through such material in a flash. It should be made of sturdy metal or wrought

iron. Glass or Plexiglas-paneled cages are pretty but severely limit the bird's opportunities to climb and exercise. They are also really tough to keep clean and presentable.

If the cage is used, be sure that the finish is not worn or chipped, allowing your pet to chew on paint flakes or untreated metal. Also, be aware that if the previous occupant died of a contagious disease, you run the risk of exposing your Amazon to the pathogen. Some virus particles can live indefinitely in cracks and crevices, even after a good scrubbing.

Is the finish safe and durable? Plated or powder-coated metals are common and usually safe, but choose a manufacturer with a good reputation to avoid potentially toxic finishes. Most cages manufactured in the United States adhere to high-quality standards. Unfortunately, plenty of imported cages are on the market. Most are good, but a few are not. Ask questions or check online reviews from other Amazon owners. If you can afford the relatively high prices, 100 percent stainless steel cages are extremely durable, easy to clean, and nontoxic. A seemingly expensive stainless steel cage might be a bargain in the long run because it should last a lifetime without the need for replacement parts. It will also delight you at cleaning time as dried food bits and bird poop wipe off with ease.

Is it designed intelligently? I recently purchased a large, wrought iron macaw cage off the Internet. I knew and trusted the manufacturer, so I was comfortable buying it sight unseen. When it arrived, I was very happy with it in almost all respects except for one glaring design flaw: the food dishes provided were only about 4 inches (10 cm) in diameter! A macaw could not possibly reach its massive beak into such a tiny bowl. The bowl certainly would not hold enough food or water for such a large bird. To make matters worse, the outside food access doors would not allow for a bigger bowl. I had to wire them shut and place large crocks on the floor of the cage. It is a really nice cage in every other way, but I wish they had put more thought into the final details. Carefully consider the usability of each feature on a cage before you purchase.

Does the shape make sense? Most popular parrot cages are basic rectangles. Some have the added plus of a cage-top play stand, which is a great place for your pet to hang out when you are nearby to supervise. Others have attractive domed tops. These are fine as long as the bars do not converge into a "V" pattern that could wedge and entrap a bird's toe as it climbs about. With a dome top, ensure that the bars are configured in a manner that allows you to hang swings and toys properly. In all cases, avoid round cages. Although they might look pretty, they deprive the bird of a safe corner into which to retreat. How much any individual parrot will be bothered by a round design is hard to gauge. Since round cages offer no benefit, why take the chance?

Consider the cage's features. Do you want outside-access feed doors so that you do not have to reach inside the cage at feeding time? This is a helpful feature if you occasionally leave your Amazon with relatives or pet sitters who fear the bird. Do you want a bottom grate to keep your pet from reaching floor debris? Or, is your Amazon one that really enjoys foraging and playing on the cage floor? Look for a cage that is designed to work with or without a grate. Do you want a cage apron that funnels tossed food back into the cage in order to keep the floor around the cage clean? I personally dislike cage aprons because they take up a lot of room. I also find them harder to clean than the floor. Besides, most of my Amazons consider it a challenge to see if they can toss unwanted food far enough past the apron to hit the floor. Do you want a playpen top, or will it sit unused because your Amazon is always chilling on the couch with you while you watch television? There are no right or wrong answers here. You should spend some time deciding what will best fit your expectations and your budget.

Cage Accessories

As a responsible owner, you must outfit a cage to satisfy all of your parrot's needs. The obvious ones are for perches, dishes, and toys. Other equally important, but often overlooked, needs are behavioral enrichment, good air quality, and proper lighting.

Perches

Most cages will come with a perch or two. You will need to add more. If you stop to think about it, a perch is a crucial bit of furniture for your pet's cage. Adult birds do not lie down to sleep, so they are on their feet virtually every moment of their entire life. If you limit your Amazon to just one or two round, hard perches of similar diameter, such as the common wooden dowel perches, it will likely develop foot or hock sores from the constant and unchanging pressure. Lack of good perches can also contribute to muscle atrophy and arthritis. To keep your pet's feet and legs healthy and strong, provide a wide variety of perching surfaces and textures.

Natural branches are great due to their varying thickness and shape. You can buy these precleaned, cut, and trimmed from most pet suppliers or gather your own from trees in your backyard. If you gather your own, you must scrub them carefully in hot soapy water and rinse them thoroughly to remove pathogens from outside birds. I then like to bake them for about an hour in an oven set at 200°F (93°C) in order to kill any possible bacteria, insects, or parasites that the hot water did not remove.

Never use branches from trees that have been chemically treated in any manner or from those that are near a busy road where they are likely contaminated with automobile exhaust.

Also be certain that the tree species you choose is safe and nonpoisonous. In general, stone fruit trees such as peach, apricot, and plum are considered potentially poisonous, as is yew. Aspen, ash, birch, dogwood, mulberry, and elm are a few common types that are considered safe. If you have any questions about toxicity, either ask your veterinarian or stick with store-bought perches.

Pedicure perches are another category that you should consider. These manufactured perches can be made from cement, terra-cotta, sand, crushed minerals, or a variety of other materials. What they have in common is a rough surface designed to keep your bird's nails trimmed down with regular usage. I have heard some people voice concerns that the harsh texture will irritate the feet, but my birds love them. If anything, pedicure perches seem to smooth and exfoliate the feet, preventing sores and cracking. Again, the key is variety within the cage.

Bendable rope perches are also a popular choice. They have the added benefit of improving a parrot's balance and grip due to the slight "give" they have under the bird's weight. They are soft on the feet, usually inexpensive, and can be bent to conform to various shapes and angles. The disadvantage of rope perches is that they can be difficult to clean properly. They also pose an entrapment hazard when they begin to fray badly. I have run these through the dishwasher to clean with some success. When they get too worn or stained, though, toss them out and buy new ones.

Dishes and Other Accessories

If you like the dishes that were supplied with the cage, purchase at least one or, preferably, two more sets. The reason is simple. On those hectic mornings when you are struggling to get out the door, it is easy to postpone changing the dirty water or filling the food dish when you have to remove, wash, and dry the old set first. If you have multiple sets, you can toss the dirty ones into the sink or dishwasher, fill a clean set, and be out the door in a flash. Also, even the best dishes might warp, crack, or wear out over time. If you have multiple dishes, breaking one will not leave you scrambling to give your bird its breakfast. Besides, the dishwasher does a much better job of cleaning and disinfecting the dishes than most people would likely do by hand.

When choosing dishes for your Amazon, stick with stainless steel, heavy-duty plastic, or with bird-safe ceramic crocks. Galvanized metal and some glazed pottery can leach toxic metals into the food and water, and are unsuitable for even short-term use. Thin plastic will not hold up to an Amazon's beak and

will soon be chewed to bits. I prefer stainless steel. The downside is that it is lightweight. A few of my birds are dish flingers. They will pick up and toss a stainless steel bowl around the cage just for fun. It makes a wonderful racket against the metal cage bars. For those birds, I use heavy ceramic crocks designed for parrots or dogs. They are too heavy for an Amazon to lift and keep the food flinging to a minimum. Be aware, however, that chipped or cracked ceramic provides a fertile breeding ground for bacteria. So replace crocks whenever they become damaged.

You will need a minimum of three dishes per cage: one for water, one for dry food (pellets, dried fruit, seeds, and nuts), and one for fresh fruits and vegetables or cooked foods. The first two dishes, water and dry food, must be kept clean and full. Captive parrots tend to graze throughout the day. They need to have a base diet and fresh water available at all times. The third dish, for wet foods such as fresh produce, can be offered once or twice a day. Moisture-filled fresh foods tend to spoil quickly—especially in warm weather. So do not allow this dish to sit out all day.

Toys

Even the best-equipped cage is incomplete without a variety of safe and fun toys. Amazons are intelligent and easily bored. They need a constant source of stimulation to keep them active and healthy. Understand that you and your Amazon might have differing ideas about what constitutes a great toy. To a parrot, a great toy is easy to destroy and makes a lot of noise. To a bird owner, a great toy lasts for a long time and keeps the bird quiet. Compromise is necessary.

sive and pretty, but they apparently were not much fun.

Everyday household items, on the other hand, such as paper (not Styrofoam) cups, empty tissue boxes, plastic straws, and cardboard tubes make wonderful chew toys with little to no expense. You can stuff cardboard tubes with pieces of broccoli, hide almonds in a tissue box, or slip matchstick-cut carrot pieces into a plastic drinking straw if you want to tempt your pet to try new foods. Foraging for food is a natural behavior in parrots and will keep your Amazon amused and busy while you are not home. Most bird supply companies sell hanging metal skewers that you can thread with chunks of fruit or veggies. You can also make your own bird-kebob with the bamboo skewers available in grocery stores. After the food is gone, your pet can safely chew and splinter the bamboo. New wooden Popsicle sticks or rolled paper lollipop sticks are available at many craft stores. You can soak them in fruit juice or flavored drink powder to add a bit of color and flavor for a cheap yet amusing chew toy.

When choosing toys for your Amazon, whether store-bought or homemade, use common sense. Do not offer your pet anything toxic or sharp, or anything that might present a hanging hazard. Amazons are playful and curious. They will easily hurt themselves with blatantly unsafe items. Be aware, however, that there is no such thing as a completely safe toy, despite some advertising claims. Parrots have an amazing ability to do the unexpected. They can find new and creative ways to get hurt no matter how innocuous a toy appears. Just do your best to choose wisely, monitor your pet's play, and remove toys from the cage when they become overly worn or broken.

Indestructible toys are usually not much fun, at least not for long. Years ago, bird toy manufacturers all jumped on the acrylic bandwagon and began churning out a huge assortment of colorful, nearly unbreakable toys. Parrot owners scooped them up joyfully, dreaming dreams of contented birds and toys that would last forever. In my case, the acrylic toys lasted about two weeks, until my birds figured out they could not destroy them. From that point on, they hung untouched in the cages, simply gathering dust. They were expen-

Behavioral Enrichment

Behavioral enrichment is a term that is tossed around a lot lately, especially by zoos and research facilities. Wikipedia defines it as "providing animals under managed care with environmental stimuli." Simply put, it means providing your pet with the tools and circumstances to keep it interested, engaged, and acting appropriately for its species. The stress of boredom can sicken a bird or cause it to act out in undesirable ways. Some bored birds will pluck and chew their own feathers. Others will develop repetitive behavior patterns, such as nonstop pacing or screaming. As an owner, providing mental stimulation for your parrot is just as much your responsibility as is providing food and water.

Luckily, due in part to their intelligence and curiousity, Amazons are pretty easy to keep amused. As mentioned earlier, having a nice assortment of toys is a great start. You can do a lot more. The following are a few ideas to get you started.

Foraging opportunities: In the wild, parrots spend a huge portion of their day foraging for food. Make your pet work a little for its treats. Use some of the ideas mentioned earlier to hide food and stimulate this natural behavior.

Visual stimulation: Amazons are extremely visual creatures and can be highly stimulated by what they see. Place the bird's cage near a window (not in direct sunlight) so that it can see the world. Consider placing a wild bird feeder in view so that your Amazon can watch the wild birds come and go. Some folks leave the television on when they are not home to keep the pets amused. Just avoid graphic or violent shows that might frighten the bird. This includes nature shows that display images of predators stalking and killing prey. In general, children's shows are popular parrot entertainment. Generations of companion parrots have grown up with *Sesame Street* and the like. Be aware that Amazons can learn repetitive words and sounds from television shows, so you might want to avoid certain cable channels!

Music to their ears: Parrots enjoy music. Like people, they have individual tastes and reactions. Some birds love hard rock music, while others might be more the easy listening type. Classical music is usually soothing, and children's tunes sometimes encourage vocal birds to attempt to sing along. I have used environmental CDs, such as the sound of waterfalls or thunderstorms, with great success in my aviary.

Puzzles: As I said before, Amazons are extremely smart birds. Give your pet toys or items that challenge its intellect. For example, I often give my parrots stainless steel bolts with wing nuts threaded on as toys. The birds have fun twisting off the wing nuts, and some will even attempt to screw them back on. Thread plastic beads onto knotted strips of leather so that the bird must untie the knots to get the bead. Make them work, and make them think.

Companionship: This is without a doubt the most important enrichment for an Amazon. I have mentioned it before in this book, but parrots need affection and physical contact. The best way to keep your Amazon happy and alert is to spend quality time with it daily. All the toys in the world would be a poor substitute for lack of human attention.

Lighting and Air Quality

Even after you have the cage properly decked out, what should you do about the surrounding environment? For your Amazon's health—and yours as well—spend some time considering the air quality and lighting of the room. Typically, people do not seem to give a lot of thought to these topics, unless they are suffering from respiratory challenges or seasonal depression. We are mobile and roam between rooms, buildings, and outdoors at will. Your bird is not and has no way to avoid dark or stale surroundings.

Air filtration: The average well-insulated house can hold air that is much more polluted than that outside a major city. It is not a matter of poor housekeeping but a matter of air circulation and exchange. Humans and pets shed skin cells and dander. Dirt, viruses, bacteria, and microbes hitch a ride indoors on shoes and clothing; furniture, carpeting, and building materials exude toxic vapors. Of course, dust and insects creep through even the cleanest of abodes. If fresh air is not allowed inside to sweep out this noxious brew, the stagnant indoor air can cause or aggravate respiratory illnesses, asthma, and allergies in both people and pets.

Unless you live in an extremely polluted area, the best way to clear the air in your home is to toss open the windows at every opportunity and allow nature to do its job. Of course, this is not always practical, especially in cold climates or for those folks suffering from seasonal allergies. The solution is to invest in a high-quality air purifier.

Air purifiers are available in sizes that range from whole-house models to small desktop versions. You must first decide how large of an area you wish to service and base your purchase on that. Consider three points. First of all, what size room is the unit rated to handle? This is usually expressed as cubic feet (cu m). So a room that is 12 feet (3.6 m) long, 15 feet (4.6 m) wide, and has a 10-foot ceiling would require a unit rated for a minimum of 1800 cubic feet (12 times 15 times 10 equals 1800) or 50 cubic meters. A few manufacturers rate by square feet (sq m). So the previous example would need a unit capable of servicing 180 square feet (12 times 15 equals 180 square feet) or 10 square meters.

The second consideration is the output capability of the purifier. This is typically rated at either "CFM," which refers to the cubic feet (cu m) of air per minute that can be processed, or "ACH," which stands for air changes per hour. Simply put, the higher the CFM or ACH number, the faster and more frequently the air in your home will be cleaned.

Finally, what type of filter system does the purifier use? The best use HEPA filters. HEPA is an acronym for high-efficiency particulate air filtration. Scientists from the Manhattan Project designed HEPA filters in the 1940s for the purpose of removing radioactive particles from the air. HEPA filters remove at least 99.97 percent of airborne particles from the air. They are widely used in hospitals and computer labs, where clean air is essential. Because HEPA replacement filters can be pricey, most manufacturers add a carbon or fiber prefilter to remove dust and other large particles and thereby extend the life of the HEPA filter. Of course, be sure to clean or replace filters as recommended by the manufacturer.

Lighting: For those people who suffer from seasonal depression, the power of light probably comes as no surprise. Light exerts a huge influence on both humans and birds. Wild birds base their lives on the length of daylight hours. It tells them when to search for food, when to begin breeding season, and when to migrate to winter habitats. Certain wavelengths of light even create physiological changes in the body, activating hormones and assisting in vitamin synthesis. Your Amazon needs light and will not be healthy or happy in a poorly lit room.

Unfortunately, providing healthy lighting is not as simple as plugging in another lamp. Basic household incandescent and fluorescent lighting is deficient in certain areas of the light spectrum and can create a sort of light deficiency. The answer is to provide your bird with full-spectrum lighting. These special bulbs are available in incandescent and fluorescent models, in a wide range of sizes, wattages, and shapes. They are designed to produce the most complete light spectrum possible in artificial lighting. They provide the closest indoor alternative to natural light. In order to be effective, they must be placed close to the bird's cage. Check the manufacturer's recommendations on placement, and use them consistently for at least 8–10 hours per day.

Of course, natural light is always uplifting. Placing your Amazon's cage in a room bathed with natural daylight through windows is great. However, be aware that window glass and plastic filter about 99 percent of light from the ultraviolet spectrum. Even in a room full of windows, your Amazon will probably still require supplementary full-spectrum lighting. Do not forget that sunlight streaming through windows can get hot! Make sure your bird can move out of the sunlight and into a shaded area of its cage if it gets too warm.

UNDERSTANDING AND TEACHING YOUR AMAZON

In the wild, Amazons forage and roost in huge flocks, sometimes numbering over one thousand birds. These impromptu communities provide better protection from predators, increased numbers to locate food sources, and cooperative rearing of fledged young. Within these flocks, their drive to form lifelong, monogamous pair-bonds truly illustrates their devotion and loyalty.

Amazons are by nature social and gregarious parrots, quick to form attachments to trusted individuals. In captivity and without a suitable mate in sight, most tame Amazons will attempt to bestow this honor upon a favored human. As we all know, humans are also quick to form strong bonds, especially with a beloved pet. This is where things get tricky.

The Bird/Human Bond

Unless we learn to speak the same figurative language as our Amazons, we are bound to stumble into roadblocks. Parrots have been kept as pets since at least the early Roman times. Despite this long-standing relationship with humans, they are still most definitely wild animals. Although aviculturists often refer to captive-reared birds as domestic, that is really

a misnomer. True domestication does not occur in a few—or even a few hundred—generations. A hand-raised baby Amazon is likely just a parent or grandparent away from the jungle and will still retain all those wild instincts and urges. The good news is that those wild urges will tell the bird it should bond with its flock mates, even if those flock mates are now human. The bad news is that without proper guidance and instruction in the ways of living with humans, the parrot will be forced to rely on instinct rather than intellect, often with unfortunate results.

For example, if a parrot spots a predator or other possible danger in the wild, it must move quickly and decisively to warn the others and chase its mate to safety. No time is available to ask nicely. Survival depends on immediate action. Usually a sudden screech and a sharp

What Your Amazon Expects From You

Because we are the smarter of the two species (although my Amazons might disagree), the human must breach the confusion and set understandable guidelines for the pet. This does not mean that the parrot does all the learning and obeying. Living with an animal, especially a wild one, is a two-way street that requires give and take from both parties. If you are looking for a slavishly obedient pet whose sole focus is pleasing you, then a parrot is not for you. If you are looking for an extremely intelligent and social animal that will usually—but not always—follow your rules, provided its own needs have been met, then you are on the right track.

Security goes far beyond the concept of food, water, and shelter. Your Amazon needs to feel safe in its environment. It needs to feel protected from other pets, rowdy children, and angry or explosive adults. Your family does not have to tiptoe about because a parrot is living in the home. However, be aware that your Amazon will pick up on the pervasive mood and react accordingly. Just as children living in a tumultuous household tend to act out, so too will your bird.

Trust: We will talk more about trust later in the chapter. Keep in mind that having a healthy relationship is impossible without trust. If you are erratic and unpredictable in your interactions with the Amazon, it will not be able to trust you. Your relationship will suffer.

Routine: Wild birds are driven by the movement of the sun and the seasons. In that world, everything happens at a predictable time: time to roost, time to forage, time to begin breeding. Your Amazon will be much happier

nip will cause the other Amazon to spring to attention and flee. The danger has been averted, and both birds live happily ever after.

Now consider the danger/flee scenario in captivity. A woman relaxes on the couch, watching television, while the loving new pet Amazon perches sleepily on her shoulder. Suddenly, in strolls that scary-looking guy with the loud voice that the woman calls "hubby." The Amazon's heart races. He must protect his new mate from this perceived threat! The parrot flings himself against her face and bites hard, hoping to drive her to safety. The woman is bloodied and upset. She cannot understand why her bird suddenly became vicious and turned on her. The Amazon, now confined to its cage, is confused, angry, and frightened. It does not understand why it has been ostracized and seethes with resentment. In one short moment, the bond has been damaged, perhaps irrevocably, simply because neither species understood the other.

if you establish a predictable routine in your interactions. You certainly do not have to rearrange your life for the bird. You should use little signals that your Amazon will learn to understand. For example, my birds know they will be fed immediately after I start a pot of coffee in the morning. I might not get up at the same time each day. However, they have learned that coffeepot equals forthcoming breakfast. If I break this routine, they protest loudly. Another important ritual is an established birdie bedtime, both to ensure that your pet gets enough sleep and to allow you some quiet time in the evening. Just be consistent, and make sure the bird has some quality family time before lights-out or cage-covering time.

Exercise: Wild parrots spend a large portion of their day flying in search of food. Your sedentary, captive bird has to shuffle only a few feet or less to a filled food dish. Because Amazons are prone to obesity, they must be allowed plenty of opportunity to exercise. Appropriate toys and play stands can help, as can certain games. One of my Amazons loves to chase. So I place him on the floor and roll a small cat ball past him. He will run after it and pounce just like a cat, albeit a very clumsy cat.

Affection and acceptance: I have lumped these two together because they are hard to separate. In case I have not mentioned it enough already, these pair-bonding flock creatures need affection and a sense of community just about as much as they need food and water. Amazons are not solitary birds. One that is kept stashed in a cage and ignored will suffer greatly. If you cannot provide for an Amazon's emotional needs, please reconsider your choice of pet.

Building and Maintaining Trust

As mentioned earlier, trust is crucial to any bond and must be established before any meaningful training begins. If your Amazon is a hand-reared baby and you are its first home, it likely has a predisposition to trust humans. The process of building and maintaining trust should be quick and easy. If your Amazon is older, wild-caught, or from an abusive or neglectful past home, you have got your work cut out for you. Even elderly wild birds can

before bringing it home. A sick parrot is probably a grouchy or frightened parrot. It will not be totally interested in companionship until it feels better.

What happens next depends on the level of tameness of the Amazon. If it is tame enough to perch on your hand without appearing stressed or frightened, then allow the bird to sit on your hand or in your lap as you watch television or read quietly. Make sure that other pets are locked in another room. Instruct family members to speak softly and move slowly while the Amazon is out of its cage. Do not let the parrot perch on your shoulder or head. Controlling the bird is difficult in this position and leaves you much too vulnerable should something startle or frighten it. Soon it will begin to relax, explore, and interact with ease. Eventually, the bird will become accustomed to the typical sights and sounds of other people and pets. It will have a much higher tolerance for normal household chaos.

If your new bird is fearful when you first acquire it, do not force it to come out of its cage until it is ready. Instead, spend as much time as possible near the Amazon without directly interacting. Allow the bird to observe you as you engage in your daily activities. Speak to it in a friendly voice, and offer occasional treats. Do not stand in front of the cage for prolonged periods. The idea is to help the bird understand that you are not a threat and that you are not interested in causing harm. As it begins to relax, it will likely call out or try to engage your attention. When it does, answer happily. Do not drop everything and run over to the cage. The idea is to build trust and a sense of belonging, not to teach the bird that you are at its beck and call.

learn to trust people. However, you will need to move slowly and give the relationship the time that it needs to develop.

Before you begin, be certain the bird is healthy. As mentioned in the chapter "Choosing a Companion Amazon," always have an avian veterinarian examine any new bird

Speech Training

Amazons are wonderful mimics and one of the most talented groups of talkers in the parrot kingdom. Does that mean your bird will definitely learn to talk? Absolutely not. Ability does not equal desire. Certain individuals never feel compelled to speak a single word of human language. Admittedly, that is rare. Most Amazons will learn to speak at least a few words. My point, however, is that you should never buy any bird based solely upon its ability to amuse you and impress your friends. You must be prepared to love it regardless of its oratory skills.

Speech training is actually pretty simple. Talk with your pet frequently, and speak in a clear and friendly voice. Parrots prefer mimicking voices that are higher in pitch and filled with emotion, instead of low, flat monotones. They will often mimic children's voices for this reason. Repeat often the word or phrase you are teaching. Do not be dismayed if your pet seems to be a slow learner. Parrots sometimes take months to learn their first word, but subsequent words come much faster as they gain confidence and skill.

Compact discs and tape programs are available that promise to teach your parrot to talk. I do not recommend them. They might work, but they just teach a bird to copy random sounds without any understanding. By working one on one with your pet, you can teach it to use certain human words appropriately. There is a debate in the scientific community about whether or not parrots can attain true language skills or if they are just very adept at applying appropriate labels. My personal opinion is that the answer depends, in part, on the intellect and interest level of each individual parrot. Most of my birds are able to label and request certain items, such as "wanna peanut" or "want water." I do have a very special African gray parrot, however, that recombines words into simple sentences and creates new labels. I am not sure if her ability meets the scientific definition of language acquisition, but she sure goes far beyond simple mimicry. Talk with your Amazon in the same manner you would talk with a human toddler, and you might be amazed at the bird's capabilities.

The Step Up Command

Once you feel that your relationship is off to a healthy start, it is time to introduce some basic skills. The most important of these is the *step up* command. Again, hand-reared babies will likely do this instinctively. It is just a matter of using the command at the appropriate time so that the bird is able to put the words together with the action. Fearful parrots, however, might need lots of repetition, patience, and praise until they begin to respond reliably.

Step up to parrots is similar to what *come* is to dogs: a means of controlling your pet's whereabouts and moving it safely from place to place. The idea is that the parrot will immediately step onto an offered hand once it hears the command. For very tame birds, it is almost a reflexive action because they want to be in the safety of their owner's hands. For fearful birds, it's a scary proposition. They are giving up their autonomy and trusting that the humans will not harm them. That is why building trust is an important first component of any training.

To begin, set the Amazon on a training stand or on the back of a straight-backed chair. Use a spot that confines the parrot to a small area; this is not the time to play chase around a huge, overstuffed chair. Place the side of your hand gently against the bird's abdomen, and say, "*Step up!*" If it obeys, praise it lavishly. If it attempts to duck backward or sideways, you can use your other hand to steer the bird gently toward your proffered hand. Be cautious. You do not want the Amazon to feel trapped or threatened. If so, it will likely bite.

If you are unsuccessful, back off for a moment, talk gently to your pet, and try again.

Key points: Keep in mind several key points. First, make sure your hand is low enough to allow the bird to step up easily. Do not hold it so high that the parrot has to use its beak to pull itself up. Second, swoop your hand smoothly and quickly against the bird while giving the command, applying gentle pressure if necessary. The trick is to unbalance the bird very slightly so that it must step up to regain its balance. Never push so hard that you cause it to fall. Instead, move swiftly and with confidence using a fluid manner. Finally, and most importantly, never jerk your hand back if the parrot reaches with its beak. It might just be reaching to test your hand or steady itself. Jerking away will cause it to fear your hand. After all, would you want to step onto a platform that abruptly disappeared every time you stepped toward it?

Biting: If you have reason to believe that the Amazon truly intends to bite, you still must never pull back. If you do, you have successfully trained it to bite whenever it does not want to obey. Instead, follow through with the command, but snap or wiggle the fingers of your other hand to distract the bird and prevent the bite. If the bird attempts to reach down and bite after it has stepped up, give it what avian behavioral consultant Chris Davis calls an "earthquake." Rapidly wobble or drop the hand on which the parrot is perching by a few inches while sharply saying *"No!"* Once again, the Amazon must stop what it is doing to regain its balance. Immediately praise *"Good bird!"*

Get down: You can also train the reverse command, *get down*, in the same session. First place your hand with the perched bird next to the training stand or chair back. Then give the command. Now slowly and gently tilt your hand toward the place you would like your bird to sit. Do not dump the Amazon onto the spot. Instead use a gentle hand tilt to encourage the bird to step onto the perch.

Choose your words carefully: Please note that you can use any word or combination of words to give a command, as long as you are consistent. Do not say, *"Step up"* one day, *"Come here"* the next, and so on. Also make each command distinctive enough so your bird can differentiate them easily. For that reason, I do not use the command *"Step off"* when I want the bird off my hand. It is too easily confused with *"Step up."* Once your pet gets the hang of these two commands, you can turn them into a game and healthy exercise by having the parrot repeatedly step up and down from hand to perch. However, do not practice training when your pet is tired, hungry, or otherwise cranky. Always try to end each session on a positive note.

Unfortunately, when training an Amazon, you will probably get bitten occasionally. If you are extremely fearful of the possibility, your bird will likely pick up on that and either become fearful itself or will exploit your fear and manipulate you. Some folks try to get around the fear by wearing gloves during the training session. However, I recommend against the practice. Gloves often frighten the bird even more, making a bite all the more likely. I can tell you from personal experience that they do not make a parrot bite much less painful.

Most importantly, never react to a bite by hitting your bird or dropping it onto the floor. Any show of anger or abusiveness on your part will immediately and perhaps permanently damage the trust between you. If you feel unsure or afraid, consider a consultation with a professional trainer or behaviorist, which is discussed in more detail in the next chapter.

Amazons have a poorly deserved reputation as being unpredictable. In actuality, they are one of the most expressive and predictable of all parrots, provided you learn to interpret their body language correctly. Your bird cannot tell you in words what it is thinking and feeling. It will, though, clearly convey those feelings through its posture, movements, and facial expressions. Spend time observing your pet. You will soon be able to understand the unspoken messages. In the meantime, here is a brief summary to get you started.

✔ **Head down, head feathers ruffled, back of the neck exposed:** This is a clear invitation for petting. Your Amazon is asking for a head scratch and a neck rub. This is a vulnerable position requiring trust, and the bird is likely relaxed and happy. One caution: Some manipulative parrots will use this posture to lure you closer for a bite. You will not likely be fooled by a familiar pet, but proceed carefully when a strange parrot appears exceedingly friendly.

✔ **Head up, feathers on the nape of the neck ruffled, beak open, bird possibly leaning backward:** Stay away. This is a threat posture, probably due to fear. Something about you is frightening to the bird. Step back, and

speak softly to reassure it. An Amazon with this posture probably does not want to bite you, but it will if you move closer or reach for it.

✔ **Head up, standing tall, feathers tight against the body, motionless:** Back off. This is a fear or startle position. In the wild, this is the position an Amazon might assume if it spotted a predator nearby. The bird is holding its breath and standing dead still, hoping the danger will pass. If you reach for a parrot in this position, it will either attempt to flee or be forced to attack.

✔ **Head up, tail feathers fanned, nape feathers ruffled, eyes flashing or "pinning":** Stay far away. This is an extremely aggressive threat posture. This is the posture that a male Amazon will use to defend his nest, and it means that he is ready to fight to the finish. Flashing or pinning eyes refer to a parrot's ability to constrict and dilate its pupils rapidly when it is excited or angry. Some female Amazons will also assume this posture, but it is more frequently used by the males. The bird might appear agitated. It will often strut back and forth in a stiff,

AMAZON BODY LANGUAGE

almost rigid manner, sometimes grunting or emitting high-pitched sounds. I have seen tame Amazons put on this display because they are excited but have no intention of attacking. However, I still would not attempt to handle an Amazon in this agitated state. This is definitely a bite waiting to happen.

✔ **Upright but slouched posture, body and/ or head feathers slightly ruffled, cheek feathers ruffled, possibly perching on one foot:** This is a relaxed and possibly sleepy bird. If the Amazon seems alert and is not excessively sleepy (heavy-lidded eyes, lots of yawns), then it might be a good time for some cuddling or speech training. On the other hand, it might just be a good time for a nap.

✔ **Ruffled head feathers, head tilted to one side, parrot touching its own face with its foot:** The bird is flirting with you. The come-hither expression is meant to melt your heart and cause you to pick up the parrot for a good head scratch.

✔ **Ruffled feathers, glassy eyes, lethargic, slouched on the perch on both feet:** This bird is likely ill, possibly very ill. See the chapter "Choosing a Companion Amazon" for additional signs of illness. Sometimes sleepy and sick look a lot alike. A sleepy parrot snaps to attention when something catches its interest. A sick bird will not look quite right, even if it tries to look normal.

✔ **Amazon crouches down, body quivers, wings held slightly away from body, head might be thrown back with beak open:** This posture depends on the age and sex of the bird. This is the posture of a baby bird begging for food. A young Amazon of either sex might also resort to begging if it is excessively tired, hungry, or insecure. This can also be the pos-

ture of a sexually mature female Amazon that is soliciting a male, or what she considers to be a suitable human replacement. If it is a hungry young parrot, feel free to give it a treat. If it is a hormonal female, ignore or distract her. Do not, however, tease or in any way encourage the posturing. Otherwise, her frustration might give way to aggressive behavior or feather plucking.

This is by no means a definitive list of Amazon behaviors. It will, though, give you a start at interpreting what your pet is trying to communicate. Over time, you will gain an intuitive understanding of its body language. Once you and your pet are in sync, you might find that you develop a nearly telepathic means of communicating. Relationships like these are not guaranteed, and they do not come easy. They require a lot of work, a lot of love, and a lot of patience. Once you get there, I think you will agree it was all worthwhile.

OUTSMARTING UNWANTED BEHAVIORS

We have discussed an awful lot about your bird's needs, but what can you realistically expect in return? Do not purchase a parrot and then try to train it to act unlike a parrot! If you are not willing to put up with some basic Amazon attitude, you will probably be happier if you stick to a more compliant pet.

Your Amazon certainly can learn some basic behavior rules, but choose your battles wisely. Amazons can be noisy birds. It is okay to teach your pet to play quietly at times, but unrealistic to expect it to keep silent from dawn to dusk.

What Is and Is Not Normal

A certain amount of vocalization (screaming) is normal for parrots, and you will not be able to change that. Amazons like to chew. The bird will not be able to differentiate between an acceptable toy and your dining room furniture. Control this behavior through supervision and by offering plenty of safe, chewable toys. Parrots bite when threatened. You will not be able to prevent bites from a genuinely frightened bird. However, your pet should absolutely learn that bullying and aggressive biting will not be tolerated.

In order to teach your pet successfully, you will need to spend some time trying to see the world through the bird's eyes. Parrots are extremely intelligent, and they do not do anything without a purpose. Your ability to guide the Amazon to good behavior will be greatly enhanced if you can get to the "why" behind the actions. You must remember, however, that parrots never act just to be bad and make your life miserable, even if it seems that way sometimes. Your pet honestly believes that its actions are reasonable and warranted. If you disagree, you need to find an acceptable compromise.

Please understand that parrots are unlike dogs. You will never be able to make an Amazon behave a certain way through force or repetition. That is why I dislike the word "training" when it comes to birds. In my mind, training implies a certain level of submission, and

that is not how bird brains operate. A dog will perform a trick to please a human; a parrot will perform a trick to please itself.

I once heard the well-known parrot behaviorist Sally Blanchard tell a story about her famous pet caique, "Spikey." Spikey performs a simple trick that involves placing rings on spindles, and he enjoys the applause from the audience. One day, he was cranky and not in the mood to perform, so he threw a tantrum and tossed all the rings off the table, much to Sally's dismay. Unfortunately, the audience laughed and applauded. Instantly, Spikey realized he could get more laughs by throwing the rings than by dutifully placing them on the spindles. So he promptly reinvented his performance. I am not sure if Sally ever did convince him to perform the original trick again.

In order to eliminate unwanted behaviors and cause real change in your Amazon, consider the following questions:

✔ What circumstance preceded the unwanted behavior?

✔ How do I imagine my bird perceived the situation?

✔ What specific action did the bird take that I would like to change?

✔ Was it acting out of fear? Jealousy? Anger? Boredom?

✔ What was the parrot's reward for its actions?

✔ How can I change the circumstances that caused the unwanted action?

✔ What will be the bird's new reward for a different, more acceptable action?

Although this sounds rather complicated, it really is not. We do these same mental gymnastics all throughout our day in dealings with other people. The process is mostly subconscious and automatic. It is all a matter of empathy. If you are aware of the fact that your Amazon is a thinking, feeling being, you will soon be able to understand and head off misunderstandings with your feathered friend in much the same way you do with human friends.

Your Bird's Place in the Flock

Parrots are flock animals. Much of their behavior in the wild depends on their position within the flock. Dominant birds get the best (usually highest) roosting spots, the most food, and usually the most desirable mates. In captivity, even domestically raised chicks will instinctively try to understand where they fit in with their human flock mates.

Height and Dominance

In an Amazon's mind, height (or control of height) equals dominance. In other words, if your pet is routinely allowed to play on top of a cage-top play stand that is above human eye level, it is the boss. This is especially true if you cannot easily reach the bird to lift it down. It is in control of its height; therefore, you must be a subordinate.

The same thing can apply to parrots allowed to play under furniture where humans cannot easily reach and retrieve them. They are in control of their height, and you are not. This is not as common but can still equal dominance in the bird's mind. Always try to keep your bird in a spot that is easily reachable and at least slightly below eye level. Of course, an occasional jaunt to the top of the drapery rod will not turn your pet into a tyrant. Allowing it to perch there on a routine basis might.

Wing Clips vs. Free Flight

This is a slightly contentious topic in the parrot community. Some folks feel that all parrots should be clipped to prevent flight, for both safety and behavioral reasons. Others believe that free flight is necessary for emotional and health reasons. Although I see valid points on both sides, I do believe that Amazons, if not all parrots, should be wing clipped. Amazons are strong, aggressive,

and excitable parrots. A free-flighted Amazon can pose a danger to humans and to itself. A flighted bird can kill or injure itself by flying into walls or windows, can escape outdoors through a briefly opened door, can fly into a toilet or aquarium and drown, can land on a hot stove and suffer severe burns, or can fly at and viciously attack a human or pet that has annoyed or threatened it.

Wing clips do not hurt and are not permanent. They are the bird equivalent of a haircut. The groomer simply clips off part of the long flight feathers on each wing. This allows the parrot to flap its wings and glide but not to attain enough lift to gain altitude. The bird can fly

down safely if it falls from a height, but it cannot usually fly upward to escape. As the bird molts and new feathers grow in, the clip will have to be repeated as needed.

A fresh clip: I can often tell when some of my birds need a fresh clip by their attitude. The most aggressive ones become nippy and bratty, knowing they can fly away and I will not be able to catch them easily. As soon as their wings are clipped, they are suddenly docile and well behaved again. Because a clipped parrot does not have the advantage of flying for exercise, however, make sure to compensate with plenty of climbing opportunities, toys, and games.

Excessive Screaming

In the wild, parrots call to keep in touch with their flock mates. In the morning, they call to announce it is time to go search for breakfast. At dusk, the flock performs a sort of roll call as they prepare to roost for the night.

You will not be able to prevent your Amazon from a little screeching throughout the day, nor should you try. Nonstop mindless screaming, however, is another issue.

Pet parrots usually scream because they want something—food or attention—or because they are bored. If your pet needs food or water, that is a no-brainer. Service the cage immediately. If it is bored, offer appropriate toys or distractions. If it wants attention, that is a little trickier. Completely ignoring a bored or lonely parrot rarely stops the screaming and might even cause worse behavior, such as aggression or self-mutilation. If you respond every time the bird yells, however, it will decide you are at its beck and call and the problem will worsen.

The key is to respond appropriately and consistently. When your parrot first screams after you leave a room, it is likely making a contact call. Respond in a calm and quiet voice, saying the bird's name and reassuring it that you are nearby. Do not return to the room while the bird is still screaming, or it will likely reason that its screaming brought you back. Once the Amazon quiets down, then return and praise the bird with a phrase such as "Good quiet bird!"

If the screaming continues longer than your sanity will hold, you may enter the room and wordlessly place a cover over the cage. Do not speak to the parrot or make any eye contact. Act calmly. You must understand that *any* interaction will be seen as a reward. A lonely parrot would rather have a human standing by its cage screaming back at it than be alone. Do not inadvertently reward the bird for screaming by saying "Bad bird" or showing any emotion. Simply place the cover over the cage and walk away. Now here is the key. As soon as the parrot stops screaming, immediately return, remove the cover, and praise the bird lavishly or offer it a treat. I know it is tempting to leave the cage covered when the bird is finally being quiet, but this will soon backfire. Eventually, it will ignore the punishment and begin to scream with even more frustration. It must learn that it is in control of the cover. "My screaming makes the cover go on and shuts me off from my flock; quieting down makes 'mom or dad' come back with a treat." Only when the parrot has some sense of control—and cause and effect—will it make the decision to act appropriately.

Biting and Nipping

Parrots use their beaks for many reasons: as a tool, as a weapon, and as a means to explore. Even tame and gentle birds will typically mouth human hands or place their beaks onto fingers to play or climb. This is not biting behavior. Puppies and kittens are commonly taught that they must never place their teeth against human skin, but once again, parrots are different. Playful grabbing with the beak is normal. Hard and aggressive biting is not. I have an African gray that loves to tussle, and she sometimes gets too rough. I just have to stop and look at her. She will then say, "OK, be gentle!" and will immediately settle down and be more careful. Learn to distinguish between unintentional nips and decisive biting.

Do not be violent: To begin, I want to emphasize that you must never hit a parrot for biting, no matter what the reason. Using violence can obviously injure the bird. Even if there is no physical injury, your relationship will be damaged. You must also determine why the parrot bit you. If it bit out of fear or self-defense, that is not a behavioral issue. Your bird is listening to its survival instincts. If your pet is simply acting like an aggressive and spoiled bully, then it might indeed need an attitude adjustment.

Stop what you are doing: Besides self-defense, the main reason that pet parrots bite is because the owner is doing something the bird does not like. The Amazon wants the owner to stop. That something might be obvious, such as teasing a bird or restraining it for a toenail clipping. It might be something subtle, such as wearing a red baseball cap that the bird really dislikes. Maybe the cause is not even the owner's fault. Parrots are masters at anger displacement. Maybe you are being bitten because the UPS driver rang the bell and frightened the bird earlier today.

Avoid the bite: In any case, the best way to deal with parrot bites is to avoid the bite in the first place if at all possible. If that sounds simplistic, it is. Learn to read your pet's body language. Do not reach for an angry parrot if you can avoid it. Of course, at times you must handle a crabby parrot, whether it likes the handling or not. At these times, your ability to remain calm and in control will help you to channel the bird's energy away from biting.

If you are bitten: If you followed the instructions in the previous chapter, you have already taught your Amazon the *step up* command. You also have a few ideas about how to avoid bites, including distraction techniques and earthquakes. What if the parrot bites anyway? The most important (and admittedly hardest) thing is to try not to react by yelling or jerking your hand away. First of all, most of the physical damage from a bad parrot bite occurs when the hand or finger is yanked from the beak. Parrot beaks are sharp. Pulling away causes a sawing action against the skin that is probably going to do more damage than the initial bite. Second, by pulling away or reacting with fear, you have just told the parrot that you understand and comply with its command. Once again, this is a reward of sorts.

Instead, quickly push the hand or finger back toward the bird as it is biting. It will not expect

TIP

Calling in the Pros

What if you still cannot convince your pet to act civil? Consider setting up a consultation with a parrot behaviorist. Like dog trainers, these folks are experts who can work with you to prevent or overcome behavioral problems in your pet, except their specialty is parrots. Check with your avian veterinarian or local bird club for referrals. Some will come to your home and work directly with your Amazon. Others will work with you through phone or e-mail consultations. Sometimes just a little extra help and support might be all you need to reach a breakthrough.

this reaction. Most parrots will immediately let go if you push toward them instead of pulling away. Accompany this movement with a sharp *"No!"* and a fierce frown to communicate your displeasure. Immediately give the *step up* command (with the other hand if necessary), and place the bird back into its cage if possible. If the bite occurred because you were attempting to remove the bird from its cage, then place it onto a chair back, play stand, or other neutral area. The parrot must understand that you are not angry and do not intend to hurt it but that you will not be bullied either. When dealing with parrot behavioral problems, always remember the three Cs: calmness, control, and consistency. Remain calm, keep control of the bird, and act consistently.

HEALTHY NUTRITION

The most common cause of death in pet parrots is malnutrition. Unfortunately, malnutrition is a sneaky killer. It rarely kills directly but, instead, weakens the bird's body and opens it to a host of other diseases and disorders.

Sometimes illness can be traced back to diet. Often, though, the underlying nutritional cause gets missed, and the parrot's illness or death is chalked up to other causes. When parrots were first kept as pets, there was no such thing as a "parrot diet." The owners simply shared whatever food they had with their animal companions.

A Poor Diet

As time moved on and bird keeping became more popular, early pet industry pioneers began to design food mixes that they deemed suitable for various species. These folks were not basing their decisions on science but on availability and palatability. Because grains and seeds were cheap, available, and tasty to pet birds, the era of packaged birdseed was born. That is what caring pet owners provided their parrots.

Not proper nutrition: Unfortunately, seed-based diets are high in fat and low in many crucial nutrients. These include calcium; vitamins A, D_3, E, K; and several of the B complex vitamins. That something was amiss became

obvious when parrots that should live 50–60 years were dying or showing signs of severe aging by their midteens. Amazons, especially, fare poorly on seed-only diets, which exacerbate their tendencies toward obesity and vitamin A deficiencies. Adding to the problem was that up until the 1980s, the only studies of avian nutrition were based on commercial poultry, which have a life span of just a few years. Finally, as importation grew and parrots became more widespread as pets, avian researchers began to take a closer look at exotic bird nutrition.

Pellets: The result of that research was the development of formulated or extruded diets, commonly referred to as pellets. Pelleted diets were heralded as a complete diet for birds, just as dry dog and cat food provide complete nutrition for those pets. Parrot magazines ran article after article on converting parrots from a seed diet to a pelleted one. Conscientious owners tossed out the birdseed and bought the pellets. Pellet diets are indeed a great improvement over seed-based feeding methods. Unfortunately, they do leave out one crucial element.

as possible, as often as possible. Think of it as a 60-30-10 diet. About 60 percent of the bird's food should come from a dry base diet. About 30 percent should be fresh fruits, vegetables, and cooked grains. About 10 percent should be treats or human food, which can include frozen pizza.

You must understand that the percentages listed are based on what your Amazon actually *eats,* not on what it is offered. Some birds will starve themselves all day, just to pig out on the much-anticipated end-of-day treats. Even though the treats comprise only about 10 percent of the food offered to the bird, they comprise about 90 percent of what the parrot actually eats. Just like we tell our kids, your Amazon must eat its veggies before it gets dessert. If you find that you are throwing out a lot of uneaten food at the end of each day, consider cutting back on the amounts fed until you reach a good balance of consumed foods.

Remember that these are averages based over time. Your bird is not going to drop dead because it ate nothing but junky treats for two solid days. It might, however, if junky treats become the mainstay of its diet for an extended period of time. Always focus on balance and common sense. If your bird overindulges on family popcorn night, that is fine. Just try to offer a few healthier choices on the following days.

Parrots thrive on variety and fresh foods, something pellets do not provide. Currently, the most recent parrot diet du jour is trending toward cooked foods and fresh fruits and vegetables. A new crop of dried pasta, bean, and grain concoctions have been designed to be cooked and served warm. If you are like me, I have a hard enough time cooking warm meals for my family on a consistent basis. I am pretty sure my parrots would wind up eating frozen pizza if they depended on my cooking.

Building a Healthy Diet

A relatively simple way is available to keep your Amazon healthy and well fed without hiring a birdie chef. The answer is to provide a solid base diet and include as much fresh food

The Base Diet

For a base diet, start out with one or more of the pelleted or extruded diets on the market. They are available in a wide variety of shapes, sizes, and colors. Some are all natural, even organic. Others are brightly colored and may contain artificial colors and flavors. Find

one that your veterinarian approves, that your Amazon enjoys, and that is easily available in your area or through Internet sources. You can mix multiple brands or stick with just one. You can also mix in a small amount of a high-quality parrot seed mix. Just keep the amount of seed small or your bird might eat just the seeds and toss all the pellets. Seeds, especially sunflower, are a parrot's equivalent of potato chips: little nutrition, lots of taste.

To create 60 pounds of the base diet, combine all of the ingredients and mix them well.

Nutrients for Your Amazon Parrot

Selected Nutrient	What It Does	Good Sources
Vitamin A (beta carotene and mixed carotinoids)	Protects skin and mucous membranes; promotes eye health; enhances immunity. Extremely important for Amazons, which are predisposed to deficiencies.	Carrots, squash, sweet potatoes, kale, cantaloupe, peaches, papaya, mango, apricots.
Vitamin C	Promotes collagen formation; enhances calcium and iron absorption; builds strong bones and blood vessels; aids in wound healing.	Red berries, kiwi, oranges, broccoli, bell peppers, spinach. Note that some bird species metabolize vitamin C in the liver, but dietary sources are still important.
Vitamin D_3	Required for calcium and phosphorus metabolism; builds bones; aids cellular energy functions.	Fish oil, egg yolks, fortified foods. Note that vitamin D is metabolized from sunlight, but indoor birds require dietary sources.
Vitamin E	Potent antioxidant; protects cells from damage; aids fertility; maintains health of red blood cells; aids immune function.	Nuts, seeds, whole grains, wheat germ, asparagus, egg yolks.
Vitamin K	Required for proper blood clotting; works with vitamin D_3 in calcium metabolism; aids in cellular energy metabolism.	Broccoli, kale, spinach, Swiss chard, parsley, turnip greens. Note that vitamin K is synthesized by bacteria in the lower intestine, but absorption can be disrupted for many reasons. Dietary sources are important.
B Complex Vitamins	Family of more than a dozen water-soluble vitamins with wide-ranging effects; critical for energy production, cell metabolism, and nervous system functions; required for health of skin, eyes, feathers, brain, and digestive tract.	Whole grains, molasses, brewer's yeast, nuts, green leafy vegetables, yogurt.
Calcium	Builds bones; critical for proper functioning of nerves and muscles, including heart; aids in blood health and clotting. Common deficiency in Amazons on a primarily seed diet.	Calcium blocks and cuttlebone, cheese, yogurt, Brazil nuts, broccoli, collard greens, kale, mustard greens, bok choy.

Keep a fresh dish of this available in each bird's cage at all times, along with fresh water. Note that the dried fruits are not particularly healthy—they usually contain added sugars or oil. My birds, though, absolutely love the taste, so they fall under the treat category.

Fresh Foods

You can get creative with fresh foods. Offer your Amazon as many fresh fruits and vegetables as possible as well as any cooked whole grains, pasta, or beans you have on hand. You can accomplish this in a few ways. If you and your family already eat a lot of fruits and veg-

gies, simply share! Make up a little dinner dish for your parrot as you prepare the family dinner, or toss some cut fruit into the cage as you prepare your morning smoothie.

If the humans in your household could use some dietary intervention as well, you will have to do a little more work. When I am busy, I often fall back on frozen or prepackaged produce. Baby carrots, frozen peas, and chopped broccoli are healthy and easily available options. If your supermarket has a salad bar, cruise through and pick up items for your pet. Red pepper strips, tomatoes, field greens, and baby spinach are all loaded with nutrients.

Some vegetables and most fruits do not require cooking. My Amazons love raw brussels sprouts and green beans. Just make sure to wash produce carefully to remove dirt, bacteria, and some pesticide residue. Be aware that juicy or highly pigmented fruits might temporarily change the appearance of the bird's droppings, making them watery or discolored. Beets, berries, and pomegranates, for example, can cause droppings to look bloody. This is normal, and not a cause for concern. Of course, if your Amazon ever has watery or bloody-looking poop combined with other signs of illness, contact your veterinarian immediately.

Organic or Not?

This is a touchy subject, and you will likely hear strong opinions on both sides. Organic is best if you can afford it, but nonorganic is better than no produce at all. Some studies have found higher levels of nutrients in organic produce, possibly because some of these phytochemicals act as natural insecticides and fungicides. Be aware, however, that organic produce is no less likely to be contaminated with food-borne pathogens such as *E. coli*. So always wash any produce carefully before eating it or offering it to your parrot.

If you cannot afford an all-organic diet for your bird, consider buying organic versions of those fruits and vegetables that are considered the most contaminated by pesticide residue. The Environmental Working Group (EWG) publishes a list called "The Dirty Dozen," which ranks the most polluted produce. This list includes peaches, apples, bell peppers, celery, nectarines, strawberries, cherries, kale, lettuce, imported grapes, carrots, and pears. By contrast, parrot favorites such as sweet potatoes,

papaya, mango, sweet corn, and kiwi are considered among the least contaminated.

Human Foods

As surprising as it might sound, your Amazon's dietary needs are not really all that different from humans'. With a few exceptions that will be discussed later, what is healthy for you is probably healthy for your parrot. The key word here, however, is "healthy." Although an occasional bite of ice cream or nibble of cake will not harm your bird, these foods add little to no nutrition and can cause obesity and malnutrition if your pet indulges too much.

On the other hand, if you cook up a mean chili filled with beans, tomatoes, and peppers, feel free to share. Some human foods are parrot favorites and can be healthy in sensible quantities. My Amazons absolutely love pizza, and a spinach pizza with whole-grain crust is surprisingly nutritious. Other parrot-healthy favorites are whole-grain pasta with marinara sauce, scrambled eggs, and cooked oatmeal with fruit. My pet birds enjoy inspecting my

dinner plate for goodies. Letting them do this is a great way to get finicky birds to try new foods. After all, if "mom and dad" are eating it, it must be good!

Foods to Avoid

Unfortunately, a few human foods can be deadly to your bird. These are mentioned in the chapter "Amazon Emergency Care."

Onions: Some reports have stated that onions (cooked or raw) in large quantities can cause a blood disorder known as hemolytic anemia in pet birds. This has been documented in dogs, but the research for parrots is inconclusive. A small bit of onion used for flavoring in a dish is safe. Do not, though, offer your Amazon onion rings or any other large quantities of onion.

═══ CAUTION ═══

Dangerous Foods
Never allow your Amazon to ingest the following:
- ✔ Avocado
- ✔ Chocolate
- ✔ Caffeine
- ✔ Alcohol
- ✔ Nicotine

Dairy: The same is true for dairy products. Parrots (and some people) lack the enzyme to digest milk sugars properly. Ingesting a quantity of milk can cause severe digestive upset. Processed milk products such as yogurt and

cheese do not pose quite the same risk, and small bits of these can actually provide a good source of calcium. Just do not let your Amazon overdo it at the cheese tray.

Dried beans: Finally, do not let your pet eat dried beans. Cooked beans are a healthy treat. However, certain dried beans contain hemagglutinins, which are substances that can damage red blood cells. Others, including lima beans and soybeans, contain trypsin inhibitors that reduce the activity of an enzyme crucial

to nutrition. Presoaking and cooking greatly reduce these compounds and make the beans safe to eat. Although cooked beans provide plenty of protein, they are missing some essential amino acids, which makes them an incomplete protein. Always pair them with cooked grains, such as brown rice, wheat, barley, oats, or buckwheat, in order to provide the missing amino acids and create a complete source of protein for your pet.

COMMON AMAZON DISEASES

Amazons are typically hardy birds and can live to ripe old ages in captivity. Diseases do exist, however. Your bird's chances of surviving will be much greater if you act quickly to get proper diagnosis and treatment.

A companion Amazon is much more likely to succumb to the ravages of a poor diet than it is to fall prey to a contagious disease. However, parrots do catch diseases at times. Parrot diseases fall into several categories; metabolic, bacterial, viral, fungal, and parasitic are the most common. Your pet's likelihood of becoming ill depends in large part on its general health and immune status, which is a direct result of the care you provide. However, even well-kept and healthy birds can become sick if they are exposed to contagious pathogens. Just as in humans, prevention is always better than treatment.

Dietary and Metabolic Diseases

As mentioned earlier, many diseases in birds (and humans) are directly related to diet. Diabetes, cardiovascular disease, and even some cancers have a dietary link that often goes unrecognized. The problem is that these diseases are stealthy and slow. We tend to not relate them back to what we eat or feed our pets. You might be surprised to learn that the dishes of fatty sunflower seeds that your Amazon loves to eat might be the root cause of its frequent sinus infections, or that the potato chips it mooches off family members are the cause of its chronic foot sores. A previous chapter discussed healthy diets. The following describes some of the disorders caused or exacerbated by poor diet.

Vitamin A deficiency, or hypovitaminosis A, is a common dietary issue for Amazons. It can manifest in a number of subtle ways. It is usually traced back to a mostly seed diet, which is highly deficient in many vitamins, including A. Birds suffering from vitamin A deficiency will usually have dry, flaky skin and poor feathering. The skin might itch or weep. The Amazon

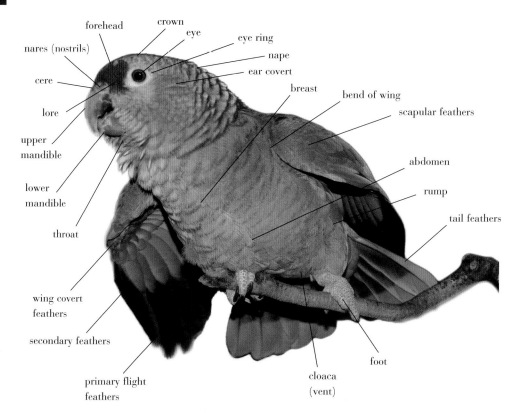

forehead
crown
eye
eye ring
nares (nostrils)
nape
cere
ear covert
breast
bend of wing
lore
scapular feathers
upper mandible
abdomen
lower mandible
rump
throat
tail feathers
wing covert feathers
secondary feathers
primary flight feathers
foot
cloaca (vent)

might chew or pluck its feathers in response. Moderate deficiencies can cause mouth abscesses, sinus and respiratory problems, and immune suppression. Over time, a chronic deficiency will likely prove fatal.

If you acquire an Amazon that shows any of these symptoms, your veterinarian will probably begin immediate treatment with vitamin A injections and possibly other drugs to treat the resultant symptoms. Of course, this is a problem that should never occur in a properly fed pet.

Although obesity itself is not a disease, it does lead to disease. Many people are surprised to hear that Amazons can suffer the same

problems as humans, including heart disease and diabetes. As in humans, obesity and lack of exercise are often the primary cause. Unfortunately, Amazons are prone to gaining too much weight and should be monitored carefully.

How can you tell if your Amazon is obese? The best way is to purchase a small kitchen or postal scale and weigh your pet periodically, perhaps once a month. Get a scale that weighs in grams, which is a more accurate method for weighing something as light as a bird. Keep track of your Amazon's weight. Consult your veterinarian if the bird gains or loses more than a dozen or so grams. Like people, a parrot's weight will fluctuate normally. Any significant changes, though, can be an early sign of disease or poor dietary choices. It is hard to tell by just looking at a bird if it has lost weight because its feathers will fill in body contours. Obese birds are more obvious. They tend to have fleshy breast tissue that protrudes along either side of the breastbone, creating what is derisively called "Amazon cleavage." If your pet has a noticeable crease down its chest, consult your veterinarian for dietary guidance and increase the bird's activity level pronto.

Bumblefoot, also known as pododermatitis, is a foot disorder frequently linked to obesity and vitamin A deficiency. Bumblefoot can range from mild inflammation to deep sores and bone infections. Improper perches, such as plain wooden dowels, can contribute to the problem, as can bacterial invasion. However, the underlying cause is often poor diet coupled with obesity. If left untreated, it can progress to severe infections requiring amputation of the affected limb, or even death.

As always, prevention is the best course. Amazons that eat a healthy diet, in a clean cage, and with a variety of perches should never be at risk. If your pet does show signs, such as reluctance to stand on one of its feet, or if you see signs of redness, swelling, or abscess, get it to a veterinarian promptly. Your veterinarian will treat the wound, probably prescribe antibiotics, and will work with you to devise a long-term plan to prevent recurrences.

Fatty liver disease, also known as hepatic lipidosis, occurs when excess calories and lack of exercise cause normal liver tissue to be replaced with fatty or fibrous tissue. Oddly, sometimes a lack of certain essential "good" fats can exacerbate the disease, coupled with an overabundance of "bad" fats. Eventually, liver function slowly declines until it can no longer keep up with the body's demands. The liver is responsible for dozens of critical metabolic functions in the body, including cleansing the body of toxins, storing carbohydrates for energy, and aiding digestion, just to name a few. Liver disease tends to move slowly and insidiously. It will eventually become fatal if not treated. Luckily, the liver is an amazingly resilient organ and can repair itself to some degree if the cause of damage is removed. Once again, poor diet and obesity are the usual culprits.

Signs of liver disease can include itching, lethargy, poor feather condition, difficulty breathing, diarrhea, swollen abdomen, and poor blood clotting. Often, the bird will not display any signs at all until the disease is well advanced. Once fatty liver disease has been diagnosed, managing the bird's diet and activity is absolutely critical. The bird must shed the excess weight and allow the liver to begin

tion might have difficulty metabolizing supplements, even those that are perfectly safe for healthy birds.

Bacterial Infections

Bacteria exist everywhere on Earth and usually coexist rather peacefully with humans and parrots. In fact, many forms of bacteria are crucial to life, aiding in digestion, synthesizing vitamins, and crowding out dangerous invaders. However, pathogenic bacteria, or those that cause disease, also surround our pets and us. In a healthy individual with a strong immune response, bacteria rarely get the better of us. Sometimes, though, the process breaks down and disease occurs.

Most bacteria are divided into two types, known as gram-negative and gram-positive. In very general terms, gram-positive bacteria are normal for parrots, whereas gram-negative are not. This is a massive oversimplification with exceptions. The majority of bacterial infections that might attack your Amazon will probably be gram-negative. Gram-negative bacteria include *E. coli* and salmonella, which are frequently implicated in food-borne disease in humans.

healing. However, you must never withhold food in an attempt to aid your pet's weight loss. Parrots with liver disease are especially sensitive to nutritional deficiencies. They can quickly become critically ill if they are deprived of food for any period. Instead, work with your veterinarian to provide a healthy and regular diet.

Your veterinarian might also suggest some supplements, such as vitamin B complex or the herb milk thistle to aid in healing the liver. Do not use anything without your veterinarian's approval. Parrots with compromised liver func-

Two methods are commonly used to test and diagnose bacterial infection. The first is known as a Gram's stain. In this method, the veterinarian uses a sterile cotton swab to collect a sample from the bird. For suspected systemic infections, the veterinarian will usually swab either the mouth or the cloaca. This swab is then smeared on a microscope slide, treated with various dyes, and examined. Due to the different ways they uptake the dyes, gram-negative and gram-positive are then easy to tell apart. This test also allows the veterinarian

to assess the relative amounts of each bacterium, in order to decide if it is a normal mix of friendly bacteria or a dangerous sign of infection.

If an infection does exist, your veterinarian might decide to run a more specialized test called a culture. Like a Gram's stain, the test begins with a swab of either the infected area or a swab of the mouth or cloaca. This swab is then run across the surface of petri dishes that contain various mediums for growing bacteria. These dishes are placed into an incubator. The bacteria are allowed to grow for a specified time, usually 24–48 hours. At the end of the incubation, the veterinarian will be able to identify clearly the specific types of bacteria to decide the best treatment option. Cultures also allow the veterinarian to test the bacteria's sensitivity to various antibiotics so the most effective one can be chosen to fight the infection.

Because so many types of disease-causing bacteria exist, listing the symptoms of a "typical" bacterial infection is nearly impossible. Systemic bacteria can attack the gastrointestinal tract, the respiratory system, the reproductive tract, or even the blood. In general, any signs of illness in your Amazon might be bacterial in origin. Your bird might instead be displaying a bacterial infection secondary to an underlying illness. In any case, prompt diagnosis and proper treatment are necessary for your bird to survive. Even mild infections can gain traction and overpower the immune system, causing sepsis, organ damage, and death.

Chlamydiosis, also known as psittacosis or "parrot fever," is caused by a small bacteria-like organism known as *Chlamydophila psittaci*. Chlamydiosis was very widespread when parrots were being imported, but it is less com-

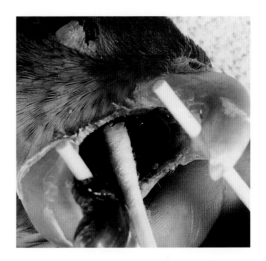

mon now. It is a zoonotic disease, which means it can spread to humans and other mammals. In parrots, it can cause mild to severe illness and death. Symptoms include depression, sinusitis, respiratory distress, weight loss, liver disease, tremors, weakness, and diarrhea. In humans, it causes flulike symptoms. It rarely causes severe disease in healthy humans but can be dangerous for the elderly or immunosuppressed. It does respond to antibiotics. However, the treatment period for birds is long, from 45 to 60 days. Amazons are highly susceptible to chlamydiosis and are likely to suffer more serious symptoms. Some pet birds, especially cockatiels, budgies, and lovebirds, can be asymptomatic carriers of the disease. So always be cautious about allowing your Amazon to mingle with these species at bird club meetings and the like. Transmission is usually through inhalation of the aerosolized feces or respiratory discharge of infected birds. If you have any reason to suspect your bird has been exposed, talk with your veterinarian immediately about beginning prompt treatment.

Viral Diseases

Viruses are small, infectious particles that can replicate only inside the cell of another organism. They are too small to be seen with a regular microscope. On average, virus particles are about one hundred times smaller than an average bacterium and can be viewed only through an electron microscope. They operate by breaking into a host cell and hijacking it, forcing the cell to aid in creating more virus particles. Because of this, viruses are tricky to treat. The challenge is to kill the virus, or at least stop it from reproducing, without killing off the host cells.

Probably the best-known viruses in humans are the rhinoviruses, which cause the common cold. Some viruses are species specific, but others can infect multiple species. Many of the influenza (flu) viruses can jump species, which

is why we hear so many warnings about bird flu or swine flu each year. Antibiotics have no effect on viruses. A few antiviral drugs are now available, and some viruses can be prevented through vaccines. In general, treatments for viral diseases are usually just supportive measures to treat the symptoms while the body's immune system fights off the intruder.

Your Amazon cannot catch your cold and is not likely to be affected by bird flu unless it is exposed to infected poultry or wild birds. However, several viruses do indeed pose a deadly threat to your pet. Remember that many viruses do not require direct contact with an infected individual. In other words, you can easily pick up viral particles on your hands or clothing if you are near infected parrots at a bird fair or pet shop and then carry the infection home. Always wash your hands thoroughly (and, if possible, shower and change clothes) after you have been near other birds and before you handle your own pets. This holds true even if the other birds appear perfectly healthy. Viruses can exist in a subclinical carrier state with no obvious symptoms. The following are brief descriptions of the most common avian viruses.

Avian pox virus was once very common in imported Amazons, especially the Blue-fronted (*Amazona aestiva*). Now that importation has stopped, this virus has become relatively rare in parrots. The disease has three forms. By far the most common—and the least deadly—is the dry form. It affects unfeathered areas such as the face, legs, and feet. It creates dry, crusty scabs and growths that can ulcerate and bleed. The growths are common around the eyes and can cause serious eye damage if not treated. The wet form is less common. It causes lesions in the mucosal tissues of the mouth, eyes, and esophagus, and it has a high mortality rate. The least common form is "acute," which causes depression, anorexia, and death.

Pox virus is spread through mosquito bites and is commonly linked to vitamin A deficiency. Treatment includes vitamin A supplementation, antibiotics to fight secondary infections, and general supportive care. Commercial vaccines are available, but they are usually recommended just for high-risk birds.

Pacheco's disease is a highly contagious and often-fatal disease caused by an avian herpesvirus. The disease tends to affect New World parrots such as Amazons, macaws, and conures most frequently and severely, although no parrots are completely immune. Some birds, especially certain conures, are thought to be subclinical carriers that can spread the disease to other birds while remaining apparently healthy themselves. Pacheco's often kills so suddenly that the first symptom is sometimes death. Affected birds, if they do show symptoms, will appear depressed and extremely ill. They might produce droppings with yellow or green urates or bloody diarrhea. The human antiviral drug acyclovir can sometimes prevent infection in exposed birds that are not clinically ill yet. However, the only treatment for sick birds is intense supportive care.

If a parrot does survive the disease, it may become a subclinical carrier that can infect other parrots. It is believed that carrier birds shed the virus when under stress. A vaccine is available. Unfortunately, it can sometimes cause severe damage at the site of the injection. Therefore it is typically recommended only for birds at high risk of contracting the disease.

Amazon tracheitis is caused by a herpesvirus but is not related to Pacheco's. Instead, it is linked to an infectious disease that affects poultry and other bird species. Symptoms include coughing, head shaking, breathing difficulties, and discharge from the eyes, nose, or mouth. Thankfully, the virus is quite rare in pet birds.

Avian polyomavirus is a highly contagious virus that is usually fatal to nestlings but rarely causes disease in adult birds. Adult birds can become infected but almost never show any signs of disease. However, infected adults can shed the virus for an undetermined amount of time and can pose a threat to any baby birds they might come into contact with at bird fairs or in pet shops. The virus was originally discovered in budgerigars (parakeets). It was known as budgerigar fledgling disease or French moult. In budgies, the disease kills large numbers of nestlings. Those that survive typically have stunted or missing feathers, especially on their wings and tails. In other parrots, exposed chicks usually die. You will not need to worry about this virus in your pet Amazon as long as the bird is weaned before you bring it home. Most chicks will not succumb to the disease past the age of about 14 weeks. A vaccine is available, but there is a heated debate in the veterinary community about the usefulness of vaccinating adult parrots.

Proventricular dilatation disease (PDD) is a horrifying disease that destroys the nerves in a parrot's upper and middle digestive tract, causing the bird to starve to death slowly no matter how much food it consumes. It can also cause damage to the central nervous system. It was originally discovered in imported macaws. It was first known as macaw wasting syndrome and then as neuropathic gastric dilatation before scientists settled on its current name. For years, its cause was elusive. In 2008, researchers at the University of California, San Francisco isolated an avian bornavirus that they believe is the culprit. Affected birds lose weight despite a good appetite and sometimes

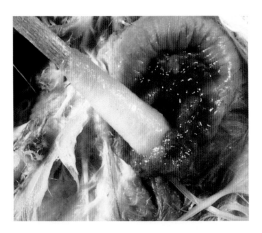

pass undigested food in their feces. Some birds will show neurological signs such as unexplained lameness, balance problems, and seizures. PDD has always been considered a disease that is 100 percent fatal. Some research with human anti-inflammatory and antiviral drugs has shown promise in treating parrots afflicted with the disease. We still do not know much about the disease. Scientists are apparently closer than ever to developing a vaccine or a cure.

Papillomavirus causes small benign tumors or growths called papillomas on the skin or mucosal membranes in mammals. In parrots, especially macaws and Amazons, papillomas are commonly found in the mouth or at the cloacal opening. Oddly, despite the similarity in appearance, researchers have been unable to prove beyond a doubt that these growths in parrots are indeed caused by a papillomavirus. They do appear to be contagious, especially between sexually active breeding birds. It has been postulated that they might instead be related to a herpesvirus, such as the one that causes Pacheco's disease. In Amazons, the growths are almost always at the cloaca and usually resemble a raspberry in appearance. Papillomas bleed easily and can cause the parrot difficulty in elimination. They can be removed surgically but usually return. Unfortunately, Amazons with papillomas are highly likely to develop pancreatic or bile duct cancer. Your veterinarian will usually check for signs of papillomas during routine exams.

Exotic Newcastle Disease (END) in parrots is caused by a virulent strain of avian paramyxovirus. The disease has several forms and can affect most species of birds. When commercial poultry flocks have END, the mortality rate is 100 percent. For this reason, international regulations strictly control the importation and quarantine of poultry and exotic birds. It is a federally reportable disease, and suspected cases must, by law, be reported to authorities. If a bird or flock of birds is suspected of END exposure, even if they are apparently healthy, they will be seized and euthanized by government agents. Because END is mostly eradicated in the United States—as of this writing, the last reported outbreak was in 2004—it is unlikely that your pet will come into contact with the disease. However, you must be very aware of the seriousness of this virus. Smuggled Amazons, especially those from Latin America, are common carriers of END. Do not ever buy an Amazon (or any other bird) that you suspect might be smuggled.

West Nile virus (WNV) has received a lot of press in recent years for its impact on humans and for its deadly effect on many spe-cies of wild birds, especially crows and raptors. West Nile is a type of flavivirus and is spread through the bite of mosquitoes. Parrots are susceptible but do not seem to be highly at risk. A few confirmed parrot deaths have been reported in outdoor aviaries in Florida. So far, the virus has affected mostly Old World parrots such as cockatiels and cocka-toos. Affected birds show mostly neurologi-cal signs. Some parrots with suspected WNV have survived and recovered with supportive care. Although this disease does not appear to be especially risky for Amazons, use com-mon sense during mosquito season. Keep your pet indoors, use tight-fitting screens on doors and windows, and remove outdoor sources of standing water, where mosquitoes breed. If you or a family member contracts the disease from a mosquito bite, you cannot pass it on to your pet through normal contact, as it is a blood-borne pathogen.

Fungal Diseases

Fungal spores are everywhere in our environment and usually do not cause too much trouble. Our immune systems—and those of our birds—are pretty efficient at fighting off these invaders. Certain things, however, can suppress your Amazon's immune response and allow

fungal diseases to take hold. These can include stress, vitamin A deficiency, poor diet, overcrowding, and other concurrent illnesses. Most of these can be avoided through proper care and nutrition. Fungal infections rarely occur in happy and well-cared-for parrots.

Aspergillosis, sometimes simply called asper, is a disease caused by a fungus in the genus *Aspergillus*, most frequently *A. fumigatus*. These spores are common and rarely cause disease until something happens to weaken a bird and make it susceptible to infection. In Amazons, aspergillosis can often be linked to a vitamin A deficiency. Vitamin A keeps mucosal tissues, such as those in the mouth, nasal cavity, and trachea, healthy and able to fight infection. Blue-fronted Amazons are especially susceptible to aspergillosis and seem to suffer the most on a marginal diet.

Aspergillosis exists in two forms: chronic and acute. Acute disease occurs when a bird is exposed to overwhelming amounts of fungi over a short period of time, such as from moldy bedding or damp, musty conditions. Signs of acute asper include loss of voice, labored breathing, weakness, depression, and sometimes lack of coordination if the spores have spread to the central nervous system. Chronic disease usually occurs in immunosuppressed birds and is sometimes less obvious. However, it can spread throughout the body and cause damage to organs and bone sinus cavities. Both forms can be fatal, sometimes with little or no preceding symptoms.

Asper is treatable. However, treatments are long, expensive, difficult, and not always successful. Once again, prevention is key. A healthy diet and clean cage will go a long way toward preventing this disease in your pet.

Candidiasis is caused by an opportunistic yeast, *Candida albicans*. It occurs most commonly in hand-fed chicks with a poorly developed immune system or in adult birds on antibiotics. Usually, the beneficial bacteria in the digestive tract keep this yeast at bay. When the friendly bacteria are disrupted or destroyed by antibiotics, candida moves in. Unlike asper, candida is usually not extremely dangerous by itself. However, it can become serious and cause damage if ignored. If a bird is on long-term antibiotic therapy, many veterinarians will automatically prescribe concurrent antifungal drugs to prevent an overgrowth of candida. Candidiasis that occurs in a bird not on antibiotic therapy, however, should always be considered a red flag for underlying illness.

Symptoms include vomiting, gagging, head shaking, a thickened or spongy crop (especially in chicks), sneezing, and difficulty swallowing. Sometimes the fungus is visible in the bird's mouth, appearing like bits of cottage cheese. Candidiasis usually responds rapidly to treatment. Mild cases can sometimes be resolved by feeding the bird probiotics, such as the healthy bacteria found in yogurt. Probiotic powders designed specifically for birds are usually available at pet shops or online bird supply retailers.

Parasites

Back in the days when parrots were imported, parasites were common and were an important topic in bird health. Today's hand-reared parrots are rarely exposed to parasites, unless they are kept outdoors in dirt-floored

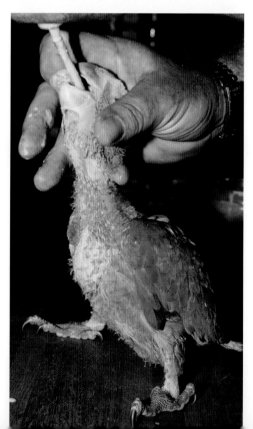

cat's fleas will not infest your Amazon. They can, however, bite the bird and cause itching or an allergic response. If your furry pets require flea treatments, be extremely cautious about using aerosol products such as flea bombs within the house, as these can be fatal to birds. Remove your bird from the house during and immediately after treatment, or seek out less-toxic treatments.

Other Diseases and Disorders

A few illnesses of Amazons are idiopathic, meaning they occur without a known cause. Sometimes the problem is a recognized disease that is simply difficult to diagnose or is presenting in an unusual manner. Sometimes the cause may be genetic or specific to that individual bird. Other times, the problem is widely recognized but the exact cause is hard to pin down due to multiple contributing factors.

Idiopathic epilepsy is a well-known disease that can occur as a result of illness, brain damage, or abnormal brain development. Idiopathic epilepsy sometimes occurs in Red-lored Amazons and is suspected to have a genetic basis. These birds might slip into a trancelike state, fall off the perch, become rigid and disoriented, or have a full-blown seizure. If you have a Red-lored that suffers from these symptoms, your veterinarian can manage the illness with drugs that reduce the frequency and severity of attacks.

Amazon mutilation syndrome: Certain parrots, most commonly Amazons and African grays, will begin to mutilate themselves for unknown reasons. They typically chew on their feet, toes, wing webs, or groin areas, causing

cages in mild climates. Parasites are typically divided into two categories: endoparasites and ectoparasites. Endoparasites include worms and blood parasites that live inside a bird's body. Ectoparasites include fleas, lice, and mites that live on a bird's body.

Endoparasites, such as intestinal worms, are mostly spread when a bird ingests worm eggs from contaminated soil or insects. Worms can cause weight loss, lethargy, poor feathering, and anorexia. Ectoparasites, such as lice and mites, are spread through contact with infested outdoor birds. These parasites can cause extreme itching, feather loss, and agitation. Again, indoor birds are unlikely ever to suffer from parasitic infections. However, your veterinarian can test for parasites if you have reason to believe your Amazon was exposed. Most parasites are species specific, so your dog's or severe trauma and infection. Some researchers believe it is a behavioral stress reaction. Others insist it is due to an infectious agent, probably a virus. To date, no underlying infectious agent has been identified. However, secondary infections commonly occur. Afflicted birds must be treated aggressively with antibiotics and will probably require some sort of collar or restraint to prevent them from reaching and reinjuring the affected area. This can be a hard habit to break. Luckily, the syndrome is rare. These birds should also have a head-to-toe physical, blood work, and dietary review to rule out obvious physical causes.

Feather plucking is a similar but much less destructive form of self-mutilation. These birds either chew off or pull out their feathers, especially those on their chest and legs. Some parrots will denude themselves completely, except for the feathers on their head, which they cannot reach. Other birds might just overpreen their feathers, leaving them intact but rough looking. Amazons are not very prone to feather destruction, but it can occur. If your pet begins to look shabby or if you see evidence of pulled or chewed feathers, bring it into the veterinarian for a complete checkup.

Feather plucking is a frustrating syndrome for parrot owners. It can stem from a myriad of causes, including stress, illness, dietary deficiencies, parasites, breeding frustration, or allergies, just to name a few. Pinning down the primary cause is often difficult. Some parrots will spontaneously stop plucking just as quickly as they began. Others will continue the habit throughout their entire life, despite repeated attempts at a cure.

As you might have realized as you read through this chapter, most diseases have multiple symptoms that overlap and can be attributed to many causes. Proper diagnosis and treatment require professional veterinary assistance and care. Please do not try to play veterinarian at home by visiting Internet chat rooms or using over-the-counter drugs. Your Amazon depends on you to provide it with the veterinary care it requires. Your well-intentioned home remedies are likely to do more harm to your already-sick pet.

AMAZON EMERGENCY CARE

When a parrot is sick or injured, immediate and decisive care is required if the bird is to survive. Amazons do their best to hide illness until they no longer have the strength to maintain the facade. You do not have the luxury of waiting a few days to see what happens.

If you followed the advice in the chapter "Choosing a Companion Amazon," you have already established a relationship with a qualified avian veterinarian. You have telephone numbers at hand for regular office hours and for after-hours emergency service. Your pet should have already seen the veterinarian for an annual well-bird check. The clinic should have all of the bird's basic information on file, such as healthy weight, diet details, and perhaps even routine blood chemistry. If you have not yet chosen an avian veterinarian, please consider doing so immediately, *before* your pet requires emergency treatment.

When to Call the Veterinarian

Sometimes the decision to call the veterinarian is obvious. Your bird has caught and broken its wing in the cage bars. A dog or cat mauled the Amazon and it is now bleeding. The bird flew onto a hot stove top and severely burned its feet. At other times, the signs are subtler and the decision is more difficult. As a general rule, if the very thought even crosses your mind that veterinary assistance might be helpful, then make the call! At worst, you will waste a few minutes on the phone while the veterinarian reassures you that you have nothing to worry about. At best, you will save your pet's life.

In my years of working closely with avian veterinarians, the one complaint I hear repeatedly is that pet owners often wait too long to call for help. By the time the bird is brought into the clinic, it is gravely ill and near death. Even if the bird can be saved, it might be facing complications and secondary infections that did not exist when the symptoms first began. Of course, veterinary bills are expensive. However, few illnesses resolve themselves or

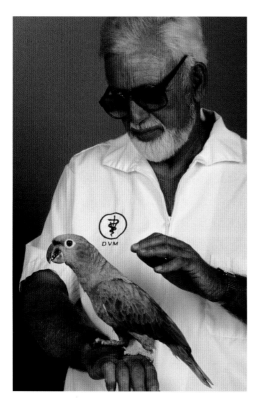

━━━━━ T I P ━━━━━

Items Needed for a Hospital Cage
✔ A rigid plastic pet carrier with a grate door on the front (designed for small dogs or cats)
✔ A heating pad
✔ Three shallow, sturdy, small crocks about 3–4 inches (7.6–10 cm) in diameter
✔ A new sponge
✔ A few old but clean towels

become cheaper to treat as time progresses. If you love your pet, get it to the veterinarian in a timely manner.

Caring for a Sick Bird

The key to caring for a sick Amazon is to get it to the veterinarian as quickly as possible. What should you do in the meantime or if a veterinarian absolutely is not available at the moment?

The first and most important thing is to assess the problem. If the bird is bleeding, burned, or has an obvious broken bone, follow the first aid procedures discussed later in this chapter. If the bird appears otherwise ill or is suffering from shock, gastrointestinal difficulties, or respiratory problems, provide heat and security.

Parrots have a normal body temperature of 105–107°F (40–42°C). Maintaining that temperature takes a lot of energy. A sick parrot that is putting all its strength into maintaining its metabolism will not have a lot of reserves left for healing. By providing sufficient warmth, you will take a huge amount of physical stress off the bird and enhance its chances of survival.

The best way to provide heat is through a makeshift hospital cage. Some books recommend placing a heat lamp on the bird's cage, but I am not a fan of that method. Heat lamps become dangerously hot and create a fire and burn hazard. Also, the heat from a heat lamp is often too diffuse to provide a consistent temperature to an area as large as a parrot cage. If your Amazon becomes too weak to perch and moves to the cage floor, it will not receive sufficient heat. Besides, a sick bird might not have the strength or coordination to navigate around its cage for food and water. It risks further injury from falling or becoming entangled in the cage bars.

A hospital cage can be made simply and inexpensively with a few common items. Simply place the heating pad on a heat-resistant surface, such as a kitchen countertop or tile floor. Place the pet carrier on top of the heating pad so that about half of the carrier is on the pad and half is not. This will allow the bird to move off the heat if it becomes uncomfortably warm. Place one folded towel inside the carrier to create a soft cushion for your pet. Fill one crock with an inch or two (3–5 cm) of fresh water and another with food. Place these into a corner of the carrier. Insert the new sponge into the third crock, add water, and set it in the carrier. This will add a little extra humidity if the bird is suffering from respiratory problems. Turn the heating pad onto the low or medium setting, depending on the ambient temperature in the room.

Finally, place the bird inside. Drape a towel over about three-fourths of the carrier to hold in the heat. Your goal should be to get the temperature in the carrier to about 90°F (32°C). You can use the draped towel to regulate the heat a bit. If the bird seems too warm (wings held away from the body and restless), fold back the towel or turn down the heating pad. If it seems chilled (feathers fluffed and shivering), cover more of the carrier or turn up the heating pad. Make sure that the heating pad's cord is safely out of reach, and monitor frequently. Do not fill the water dish with more than an inch (2.5 cm) or so of water, and do not use deep or wide crocks. If your Amazon loses consciousness or becomes disoriented,

it could fall forward and drown in a large or deep dish.

Of course, this is a makeshift and temporary solution. Do not leave a sick bird unattended or leave the house with the heating pad on. This is intended to provide only supportive care until you can safely transport your pet to the veterinary clinic. The advantage of using a pet carrier as a hospital cage is that you can simply pick it up and carry it to your car (preheated if the weather is cold!) when it is time to leave for the veterinarian. Your Amazon will be secure and warm and will not be stressed by excess handling.

Emergency First Aid

What if your Amazon is not sick but has been injured? You will still need to follow the above instructions and get it to the veterinarian as quickly as possible. However, you might need to take some extra steps first. The following are some common scenarios.

Bleeding

First determine the cause and the location of the bleeding. Is it a large wound, such as from an animal bite, or a localized spot, like a broken toenail? If another animal bit the bird, it will need to go to the veterinarian even if the bleeding is minor. It might have internal injuries from the crushing pressure of the bite, and it will definitely need antibiotics. Cats especially carry a bacterium in their saliva (*Pasteurella*) that is absolutely deadly to birds.

Even a tiny accidental scratch from a friendly and playful cat can introduce these bacteria into a bird's bloodstream and cause a fatal systemic infection.

If the wound is large, hold gentle pressure with a square of sterile gauze until the bleeding has stopped. Birds have very little blood volume, so even a relatively small loss is enough to cause shock. If the bleeding is not severe, you might wish to flush the wound with water, hydrogen peroxide, or sterile saline solution. Then dab it with a povidone iodine solution, such as Betadine. This is a safe antiseptic and antimicrobial agent that will kill many germs. It is also easy on skin tissue.

Do not attempt to bandage the wound with regular first aid tape. Most human bandaging materials have adhesives that will severely damage the parrot's feathers and perhaps its skin as well. If you must use something to hold the gauze in place, use a stretchy self-adhesive bandage such as Vetrap (available from your veterinarian or some pet shops). Wrap it just tightly enough to hold but not so tight as to cause your bird distress. Transport the bird immediately to the veterinarian for further treatment.

For minor bleeding caused by broken nails or feathers, first do what you can to calm the bird. Sometimes, these minor injuries will coagulate and heal without assistance if the parrot is allowed to calm down. Stress and fear increase the heart rate and will only make the wound bleed faster. Turn down the lights, kick other family members and pets out of the room, and quietly observe for a few minutes. If the bleeding is very slow, just a small drop or two every minute, wait a few minutes to see if it stops on its own. If it does not stop within minutes or if the bleeding is rapid, you will need to intervene.

For broken toenails or chipped beak tips, use a styptic powder, which is available at pet shops. These coagulant powders will usually stop bleeding almost immediately when the powder is pressed against the bleeding spot. If you do not have styptic powder, flour or corn-

starch will work but not as quickly or as well. Regular styptic powder can sting. However, some newer versions include the topical anesthetic benzocaine to relieve pain. You can also use this on very tiny cuts. It is not designed for use on larger wounds and should never be used for that purpose.

Broken blood feathers: Another common cause of bleeding in parrots is broken blood feathers. When growing flight feathers emerge through the skin of the wing, they are encased in a keratin sheath that is filled with blood. As the feather develops, the blood gradually recedes and the sheath crumbles off to reveal the new feather. If one of these feathers is broken while the blood is still present, it can bleed badly. Sometimes they stop bleeding without intervention, especially if the feather is mostly grown. Often they do not. When this happens, it is not always obvious that the problem is from a wing feather. Usually, the first place you will notice blood is on the bird's flank or thigh, where the wing has rested. If

you take a close look at the underside of the wing, however, you should be able to spot the broken and bleeding feather shaft.

When a blood feather does not stop bleeding on its own within a few minutes, the only way to stop the bleeding is by pulling out the broken feather. Otherwise, the broken shaft will act as a wick and keep drawing blood from the bird's body. You will need a towel, a pair of needle-nosed pliers, some styptic powder, and an assistant. Pulling a blood feather from a parrot as large as an Amazon is a two-person job. One person must gently restrain the bird in a towel, while the other carefully unfolds the wing and locates the bleeding feather. Use one hand to grasp the top of the wing nearest the feather firmly. With the other hand, use the pliers to grasp the feather shaft as close to the skin as possible. In a quick and fluid motion, pull the shaft in the direction of growth.

This does hurt, and your bird will be upset and angry or frightened. Always make sure the person doing the restraining knows the proper technique and does not release the parrot until you are completely done. Otherwise you risk a nasty bite. After you have pulled the feather, hold gentle pressure on the spot for a minute or two to prevent bleeding from the follicle. If it does bleed, a little styptic powder should help it stop. Feather follicles rarely bleed profusely or for any length of time once the broken shaft is removed. Once you are sure the bleeding has stopped, the person restraining the Amazon should carry it back to the cage and release it *into the cage*. Do not try to handle the bird immediately after this procedure. It will not be a happy camper, and you will likely end up needing some styptic powder yourself.

Burns

Most burns in parrots occur on the feet. The bird flies onto a hot stove, steps on a lit cigarette, or reaches for a candle. Burns can also occur in the mouth if a parrot bites an electrical cord. Always try to keep your pet safe from such hazards. If one does happen, you must quickly assess the severity and size of the burn. If the burned area is on the feet or legs, immediately stand the bird in a dish of cool (not cold) water for several minutes. You can also use a squirt bottle filled with cool water to flush the burn and prevent further damage. If it is a minor burn—the skin is reddened but not peeling or blistered—you can gently apply a water-based antibiotic ointment such as Thermazene, a silver sulfadiazine cream. Apply the cream twice a day. Call your veterinarian if the burn begins to look worse or if the bird appears ill. Never use oil-based ointments, which can destroy feathers and might be toxic to your pet.

If the burned area is large or severe, with blistering, bleeding, or peeling skin, it is an emergency that requires immediate veterinary assistance. The Amazon might go into shock and will require antibiotics and possibly intravenous fluids. Do not attempt to treat at home severe burns or any burns in or around the mouth or eyes.

Broken Bones

Amazons are rowdy. They can get tangled up in a toy and break a wing. Sometimes birds get stepped on or accidentally caught in a closing door. A free-flighted parrot might slam into a window or mirror, breaking bones or suffering a concussion. Broken bones are always an emergency and require immediate veterinary attention. Place the bird into the heated hospital cage described earlier in this chapter to limit its motion and prevent shock. You can pad the carrier with extra towels for

comfort. Do not attempt to splint or bandage a broken bone on your own. You may very possibly injure your pet further.

Poisoning

The most critical first action is to attempt to identify the source of the poison. For inhaled toxins such as Teflon fumes or aerosol products, immediately rush the bird into an area of fresh air. If possible, quickly place it into its pet carrier, and bring it outdoors while you allow the house to ventilate fully. Even a brief exposure to bitterly cold fresh winter air will be less harmful than remaining indoors with the source of toxicity. A parrot in respiratory distress needs immediate veterinary attention. Even if the fresh air seems to revive the bird, it will probably require drugs to prevent later swelling, inflammation, and infection in its respiratory system.

For ingested toxins, try to figure out what the Amazon ate. Parrots are like toddlers, and everything seems to wind up in their mouths. If you can identify the poison, call your veterinarian or the National Animal Poison Control Center at 1-888-4ANI-HELP (1-888-426-4435). There is a charge for the service. However, the veterinary toxicologists who answer the phone will work with you or your veterinarian to find the safest resolution. Although some poisons are obvious, such as rat poison, household chemicals, and pesticides, there are plenty of substances toxic to birds that you might not suspect. The following are all potentially poisonous to your Amazon:

✔ Cigarette butts or any other form of nicotine
✔ Alcoholic beverages
✔ Caffeine
✔ Avocados
✔ Chocolate
✔ Salty snacks
✔ Certain houseplants
✔ Lead from stained-glass items
✔ Matches

To keep your pet safe, always closely monitor out-of cage time. Keep potentially dangerous items out of reach. A determined and intelligent Amazon can be a mighty force to reckon with when it spots something that it wants. So offer plenty of safe alternatives for play and treats.

A parrot survival kit consists of three main parts: emergency first aid supplies, a carrier/hospital cage, and important documents. Find a safe and convenient place to keep these supplies, preferably close to your pet's cage. You do not want to be rummaging in the garage while your bird is in distress at the other end of the house. You can spend a lot and make a fancy kit or buy the bare minimum and store it in an old box. Try to acquire as many of these items as possible.

Emergency First Aid Supplies

To begin, buy a waterproof plastic container to corral all the supplies. I use a medium-sized plastic toolbox. However, fishing tackle boxes, craft bins, and plastic shoeboxes work as well. For items with a limited shelf life, like ointments and wound cleansers, buy the smallest size available. Trial or travel sizes are great if you can find them. Here is a basic list of what you should include in your kit:

✔ Gauze squares
✔ Cotton balls and cotton-tipped swabs
✔ Stretchy self-adhesive bandaging tape such as Vetrap
✔ Needle-nosed pliers, locking forceps, or hemostats to pull blood feathers
✔ Blunt-edged scissors for clipping wings or cutting bandages
✔ Nail clippers (small dog or cat nail clippers work well for birds)
✔ Small flashlight with batteries
✔ Magnifying glass
✔ Towel for restraint
✔ Heating pad

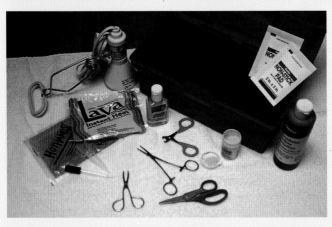

✔ Eyedroppers or syringes (without needle) for administering medication or fluids
✔ Pedialyte or other oral rehydrating agent
✔ Sterile saline solution
✔ Hydrogen peroxide 3% solution
✔ Betadine or other povidone iodine solution
✔ Thermazene or other water-based antibiotic ointment
✔ Hand sanitizer (use before handling an injured or ill bird)
✔ Styptic powder
✔ Aloe vera gel for mild burns or skin irritations
✔ Small jar(s) of human baby food or baby bird hand-feeding formula for feeding sick birds
✔ Postal or kitchen scale for monitoring weight

Travel and Hospital Cage

Rigid plastic pet carriers designed for dogs and cats make wonderful carriers for parrots. Choose a size large enough for your Amazon to sit inside and move about comfortably, including room for food and water dishes.

Some of these carriers are designed with top grates, but I prefer those with front grates. The front grates allow the bird to see outside, but still feel protected. Also, most parrots will hold onto a front grate with their beaks or feet if they need to steady themselves during travel.

If you are handy with a drill and saw, it is easy to add a perch to the carrier. Simply measure and cut a wooden dowel the width of the carrier a few inches from the bottom. Drill a hole through the plastic sides where you want the perch to sit. Hold the perch in place, and place a screw through the hole and into the perch on each side. It needs to be only a few inches off the floor so that your pet has room to arrange its tail feathers comfortably. Be sure to leave enough room above so that the bird does not have to sit hunched over.

Once you have set up this travel cage, place a towel, a few small crocks, some bottled water, and a small waterproof container of your bird's usual dry food inside, preferably confined into one or two plastic zip-top bags. If you are ever forced to evacuate your home due to fire or other sudden emergency, you can rapidly place your pet inside and evacuate quickly and safely. I always recommend that you place your name and telephone number and the name and phone number of your veterinarian on the carrier with either a waterproof label or indelible marker in case you and your parrot are separated in a crisis. You can also purchase a personalized dog tag at many pet shops and simply attach it to the carrier's grate or handle.

Important Documents

Now you need to make sure you have certain information at your fingertips to put those supplies to good use.

To begin, gather all the emergency telephone numbers that might come in handy. Always keep a pen and notepad with your other supplies in case you need to write down instructions from your veterinarian. Important phone numbers include:

✔ Your avian veterinarian's regular and after-hours numbers
✔ Nearby emergency veterinary clinics
✔ 24-hour Animal Poison Control Hotline
✔ Police nonemergency number to report if your bird is lost
✔ Area shelters, humane societies, and pet shops to call if your bird is lost
✔ Contact information for local bird clubs that can offer advice and support when needed
✔ Local bird sitters or bird-boarding facilities
✔ If you are traveling with your bird, locate an avian veterinarian in your destination city and carry the name and address along with you

In addition to the telephone list, keep a record of your Amazon's history in case you need to visit a veterinarian who has not seen your bird before. Write down items such as the bird's age, sex if known, band or microchip number, typical diet, average weight, past medical problems and vaccinations.

Finally, take a few clear digital photos of your pet from different angles. If your bird has any distinguishing characteristics, such as missing toes, be sure to document this in photos. If your Amazon is ever lost or stolen, these photos can be used on missing posters and may be used to prove ownership of a stolen bird.

SELECT AMAZON SPECIES

Before you can understand how Amazons are classified into species, you should have at least a vague understanding of how taxonomy works.

Taxonomy is the science of classifying organisms into hierarchical groups. It helps scientists clearly isolate exactly which organism they wish to discuss or study. Unfortunately, taxonomy changes frequently, and classifications can get reshuffled. That is why it is impossible to declare categorically exactly how many species of Amazons exist. The birds themselves do not appear or disappear in any manner. Instead, the manner in which they are classified changes.

Taxonomy Review

You can visualize taxonomy as a ladder, with each descending rung representing a smaller and more closely defined group. At the top of the Amazon parrot ladder is the kingdom: Animalia. This tells us that Amazons are animals, as opposed to plants. Next is the phylum: Chordata. This tells us they are animals with a spinal cord. Next is class: Aves. This class includes all birds. After class comes order: Psittaciformes. This order includes all parrots. Next is family: Psittacidae. Psittacidae includes all parrots except cockatoos and New Zealand parrots, which branch off into their own group

at this juncture. Family is then broken down into smaller groups called subfamilies and/or tribes. Depending on the source you consult, Amazons are described as either subfamily Psittacinae or Arinae and as tribe Arini.

After tribe is genus. All Amazon parrots belong to the genus *Amazona.* Here is where the taxonomy really starts to get confusing. After genus is species and then subspecies. This is where taxonomists often tend to disagree. It is not uncommon to see a particular Amazon listed as a species in one book, as a subspecies in another, and as merely a color variation of the nominate (main) species in a third!

This chapter offers a general description of some of the most common Amazons, using the most common classification at the time of this writing. Some species, such as the Yellow-crowned *Amazona ochrocephala,* are undergoing current scientific disputes regarding their classification. So it is entirely possible that you will find other sources containing differing information. That's part of what makes taxonomy so interesting. Scientists are now using DNA to help them re-sort and shuffle various species, but I suspect we are still a long way from the final answer.

Common Amazon Species

Blue-fronted Amazon
Amazona aestiva

The Blue-fronted Amazon is perhaps the most widely distributed Amazon in the pet trade. It is a large and attractive parrot known for its excellent talking ability. Wild Blue-fronts are found throughout much of Brazil, Bolivia, and parts of northern Argentina and Paraguay.

Description: Forehead and lores are bright turqouise blue; the crown and area surrounding the eyes is yellow. In the nominate species, the bend of the wing is mostly red with some yellow feathering. Subspecies *xanthopteryx* (sometimes called the Yellow-winged Amazon) tends to be larger. The wing bend is primar-

ily yellow, sometimes extending far down the top of the wing. Feet and legs are dark gray, and the beak is blackish gray. Prominent black eyelashes. The green feathers on the nape and neck are sometimes edged with black, giving a scalloped appearance. The amount of blue and yellow is quite variable on Blue-fronts. Some birds have almost solid yellow faces with just a trace of blue, and others are mostly blue with little yellow. The Amazona Society breaks them into two types of the nominate species and two types of the *xanthopteryx* subspecies.

Orange-winged Amazon
Amazona amazonica

The Orange-winged Amazon is another common pet. It is often confused with the Blue-fronted, which it resembles at first glance and whose range it overlaps in some areas. Orange-wings are widely distributed across much of central and northern South America and are probably the least-endangered Amazon species.

Yellow-headed Amazons
Amazona ochrocephala Group

As mentioned earlier, *Amazona ochrocephala* is a species that is currently wracked with confusion. The Amazona Society lists a total of 15 species and subspecies of *A. ochrocephala.* Aviculturist Rosemary Low lists 10 but is quick to point out the difficulty of separating the various races. Researcher Tony Jupiter recognizes four subspecies of *ochrocephala* but breaks out four more under the species *Amazona oratrix* and an additional three under the species *Amazona auropalliata.* Confused yet?

This group encompasses a widespread distribution of Amazons that range from Mexico

They can make wonderful and affectionate pets, although they tend to be slightly more shy than Blue-fronts and do not always gain the same vocabulary.

Description: Orange-wings are usually smaller than Blue-fronts, and the blue on their forehead is a deeper bluish purple. The yellow on their face is typically confined to the area under their eyes and is often tinged with a light orange wash. Beak is horn colored with a grayish black tip; legs are gray. Overall green is often somewhat duller than in the Blue-fronted, but individual colors can vary considerably.

down through central South America. In many areas, the ranges overlap. Telling which populations constitute discrete species, closely related subspecies, or perhaps even partially hybridized groups is difficult. In general, they are large Amazons with mostly green bodies and widely varying amounts of yellow on their faces, heads, or bodies. They are typically boisterous birds with excellent talking ability.

Descriptions and common names:

✔ Yellow-crowned Amazon, *Amazona ochrocephala ochrocephala,* also known as the Yellow-fronted Amazon: forehead bright yellow, beak dark gray with reddish cast on upper mandible; legs gray.

✔ Marajo Yellow-headed Amazon, *Amazona ochrocephala xantholaema:* similar to the Yellow-crowned but more extensive yellow on the face, usually surrounding the eyes and reaching back to hind crown; bluish tinge on breast.

✔ Natterer's Amazon, *Amazona ochrocephala nattereri:* face mostly bluish green, with a small band of yellow on crown; bend of wing red, sometimes mixed with yellow.

✔ Panama Yellow-headed Amazon, *Amazona ochrocephala panamensis:* V-shaped patch of yellow on forehead, prominent eye ring; beak is horn colored.

✔ Yellow-naped Amazon, *Amazona ochrocephala auropalliata:* face is a pale bluish green, sometimes with a narrow yellow frontal band; broad band of deep yellow feathers across the nape; nares black, and beak is black to slate colored; large whitish gray eye ring.

✔ Parvipes Yellow-naped Amazon, *Amazona ochrocephala parvipes:* similar in coloring to the nominate race but smaller in size; also distinguished by red feathers on bend of wing and lighter-colored beak.

✔ Roatan Yellow-naped Amazon, *Amazona ochrocephala caribeae:* similar to *A. o. parvipes,* but beak is lighter still and green feathers have a more olive green cast; immature birds might not show any yellow.

✔ Double Yellow-headed Amazon, *Amazona ochrocephala oratrix:* bright-yellow head and nape, sometimes mixed with green feathers on neck; bend of wing red or red/yellow; pale horn-colored beak, legs gray; immature birds mostly green; full yellow head does not develop until about 4 years of age.

✔ Tres Marias Amazon, *Amazona ochrocephala tresmariae:* slightly larger than the Double Yellow-headed and with more extensive yellow extending down neck and throat; green underparts are tinged with blue; sometimes has red feathers mixed in with yellow head feathers; legs and nails are pink, beak is light ivory.

✔ Belize Double Yellow-headed Amazon, *Amazona ochrocephala belizensis:* less yellow on head, none on throat; yellow is confined to face and crown; usually smaller than nominate Double Yellow-headed.

✔ Greater (Magna) Double Yellow-headed Amazon, *Amazona ochrocephala oratrix:* largest of the species and most yellow in feathering; yellow head and neck, yellow sometimes extending well into the upper breast, sometimes mixed with red; shorter tail than other subspecies; pinkish ivory beak and legs.

Green-cheeked Amazon
Amazona viridigenalis

The Green-cheeked Amazon, also known as the Mexican Red-headed, is a medium-sized, stocky Amazon that can usually be found in

feathers on upper back, and chest sometimes tipped with black. Yellowish horn beak; light gray legs.

Lilac-crowned Amazon
Amazona finschi finschi

The Lilac-crowned is sometimes confused with the Green-cheeked Amazon, but Lilac-crowns are smaller and less stocky. They are relatively shy and quiet for Amazons. However, they still maintain the Amazon personality. They inhabit the Pacific coast of Mexico. Some feral birds have been reported in the United States. Status in the wild is near threatened.

Description: Forehead and lores are a darker, duller red than in Green-cheeks. Feathers on the crown and neck are lilac, sometimes edged with black. Lower neck and mantle green edged with black, giving a scalloped effect. Legs medium gray; beak is horn colored.

Red-lored Amazon
Amazona autumnalis autumnalis

The Red-lored Amazon, also known as the Yellow-cheeked Amazon, ranges from Mexico through Central America and into northern South America. Three subspecies are recognized. However, the nominate species was the most frequently imported and is the most common in aviculture. It inhabits a wide range of ecosystems and is somewhat nomadic, moving from rain forests to open habitat after breeding season.

Description: Forehead and lores deep red, bright yellow-orange cheeks, crown lilac blue. Nape and neck green to lilac, tipped with black. Prominent white eye ring and black eyelashes. Gray legs, lower mandible gray, and upper mandible horn tipped with dark gray.

the pet trade. It inhabits northeastern Mexico, but some feral populations are in California and Florida. It is nomadic and sometimes appears in southwestern Texas during winter season.

Description: Bright scarlet red forehead and lores, with violet blue feathering on hind crown. Bright-green cheek feathers. Green

Description: Distinctive red, white, and blue coloring of head. White forehead with deep-blue crown, red mask around eyes. Prominent white eye ring. Beak is pale yellow; legs are pinkish gray. This species is considered dimorphic, with males having red on the primary wing coverts and females having green. Additionally, males' faces have a greater degree of red. Rosemary Low notes that exceptions exist, and a few proven hens have shown coloration typical of males.

White-fronted Amazon
Amazona albifrons albifrons

The White-fronted Amazon, commonly known as the Spectacled Amazon, is one of the smallest Amazons. The two recognized subspecies are *Amazona albifrons saltuensis* and *Amazona albifrons nana*. The *nana* subspecies differs mostly in size from the nominate. For this reason, the nominate race is sometimes referred to as the Greater White-fronted and the *nana* subspecies as the Lesser White-fronted. They range from the Pacific coast of Mexico down through parts of Central America, as far as Costa Rica.

INFORMATION

Periodicals

The AFA Watchbird
American Federation of Aviculture, Inc.
P.O. Box 91717
Austin, TX 78709-1717
(512) 585-9800
www.afabirds.org/watchbird.shtml

Bird Talk/Birds USA
P.O. Box 6050
Mission Viejo, CA 92690
(949) 855-8822
www.birdchannel.com

Organizations

The Amazona Society
7404 Washington Avenue S.
Eden Prairie, MN 55344
www.amazonaonline.com

American Federation of Aviculture
P.O. Box 91717
Austin, TX 78709-1717
(512) 585-9800
www.afabirds.org

Association of Avian Veterinarians
P.O. Box 811720
Boca Raton, FL 33481
(561) 393-8901
www.aav.org

Helpful Websites

www.avianweb.com
www.birdchannel.com
www.upatsix.com

Manufacturers and Suppliers

Cage Catchers
Div. of Handy Wacks Corp.
100 E. Averill Street
Sparta, MI 49345
(800) 445-4434
www.cage-catchers.com
(custom-made cage bottom liners)

Kaytee Products, Inc.
521 Clay Street
Chilton, WI 53014
(800) 669-9580
www.kaytee.com
(seed, formulated diets, and treats)

L'Avian Pet Products
Highway 75 S
P.O. Box 359
Stephen, MN 56757
(800) 543-3308
(L'Choice bird diets)

Pretty Bird International, Inc.
31010 Foxhill Avenue
P.O. Box 177
Stacy, MN 55079
(800) 356-5020
www.prettybird.com
(seed, formulated diets, and treats)

Prevue Pet Products, Inc.
2700 West Fulton Street
Chicago, IL 60612-2004
(800) 243-3624
(pet and breeding cages)

Rolf C. Hagen U.S.A. Corp.
50 Hampden Road
Mansfield, MA 02048
(800) 225-2700
www.pubnix.net/~mhagen
(various bird products, seed diets)

Roudybush
340 Hanson Way
Woodland, CA 95776
(800) 326-1726
www.roudybush.com
(pelleted diets)

About the Author

Gayle Soucek has been keeping and breeding a variety of exotic birds for over twenty years. She is the author of seven books and numerous magazine articles on avian husbandry, nutrition, breeding, and disease, and is a contributing writer for www.webvet.com. Gayle is past-President of the Midwest Avian Research Expo, the Midwest Congress of Bird Clubs, and the Northern Illinois Parrot Society, and is a current member of the Amazona Society. She resides near Chicago with her husband, birds, dogs, and one very laid-back cat.

Photo Credits

Joan Balzarini: pages 27, 28, 42, 48, 53, 56, 57, 77, 87 (bottom), 88 (top, bottom), 91; Norvia Behling: pages 51 (top), 55, 72; Gerry Bucsis and Barbara Somerville; Parrots courtesy of Bird Kingdom, Niagra Falls, ON: pages 4, 6, 10, 25, 30, 40, 41, 49, 86 (top, bottom), 87 (top); Shirley Fernandez: pages 9, 93; Isabelle Francais: pages 5, 13, 19, 20, 22, 36, 37, 39, 59, 65, 73, 75, 76, 89; Paulette Johnson: pages 16, 18, 45, 58, 67, 68 (bottom), 69, 70, 74, 79, 91; Dr. Scott McDonald: pages 62 (top, bottom), 63, 66; Pets by Paulette: pages 17, 31, 85; Pete Rimsa: pages 38, 44, 46, 51 (bottom), 60, 61, 71, 78, 81, 82, 83; Shutterstock: pages 2–3, 8, 15, 35, 43, 50, 54, 64, 80, 84, 90; Connie Summers: pages 7, 11, 12, 14, 21, 24, 26, 32, 33, 34, 68 (top).

Cover Photos

Shutterstock: front cover, back cover, inside front cover, inside back cover.

Important Note

Please remember that Amazons are intelligent and endangered birds. They require a substantial amount of care, and are not low maintenance pets. They should never be purchased on a whim. If you are ever unable to care for your Amazon, please contact a local bird shelter for guidance. Releasing a nonindigenous bird into the wild is against the law in most states, and it is unlikely a domestically raised Amazon could survive outdoors.

Acknowledgments

The author would like to thank the Amazona Society and all the individuals it encompasses for their tireless work on behalf of genus *Amazona*, and the invaluable education they offer. I'd also like to thank my patient and talented husband, Pete, for his generous assistance and photography skills. And finally, thanks to Lorena, Dan, Barb, and Flo for the support and encouragement.

All inquiries should be addressed to:
Barron's Educational Series, Inc.
250 Wireless Boulevard
Hauppauge, NY 11788
www.barronseduc.com

Library of Congress Catalog Card No. 2010011079

ISBN-13: 978-0-7641-4341-0
ISBN-10: 0-7641-4341-7

Library of Congress Cataloging-in-Publication Data
Soucek, Gayle.
    Amazon parrots : a complete pet owner's manual /
By Gayle Soucek.
        p. cm.
    Includes bibliographical references and index.
    ISBN-13: 978-0-7641-4341-0 (alk. paper)
    ISBN-10: 0-7641-4341-7 (alk. paper)
    1. Amazon parrots. I. Title.
    SF473.P3S654 2010
    636.6'865—dc22   2010011079

Printed in China

9 8 7 6 5 4 3 2 1